THE WILL IN HUMAN LEARNING

THE WILL IN HUMAN LEARNING

by

Russell A. Peterson

GRAPHIC PUBLISHING COMPANY, INC.

THE WILL IN HUMAN LEARNING

Copyright by Russell A. Peterson
1977

Library of Congress
Catalog Card No.: 77-82599
ISBN: 0-89279-007-5

Printed by
Graphic Publishing Company, Inc.
Lake Mills, Iowa 50450

FOR MY

COLLEAGUES

IN THE

CENTER FOR TEACHING and LEARNING

THE

UNIVERSITY OF NORTH DAKOTA

BOOKS and TRANSLATIONS

by

Russell A. Peterson

Translations

The God that Job Had
The Synoptic New Testament
Reading the Psalms
Children's Tales From Norway

Books

The Size of Death
Education is a Philosophy
Campus Invocation
Existentialism and the Creative Teacher
Counseling Tips for the Beginning Teacher
Luther For Today
How Love Will Help
Lutheranism and the Educational Ethic
God and I
An Introduction To Theory of Knowledge
A Dictionary of Philosophical Concepts
The Will in Human Learning

CONTENTS

CHAPTER ONE
    Mental Behavior   11

CHAPTER TWO
    Moral Authority   45

CHAPTER THREE
    Freedom   55

CHAPTER FOUR
    Choice   87

CHAPTER FIVE
    Determinism 103

CHAPTER SIX
    Decisions 125

BIBLIOGRAPHY 131

INTRODUCTION

Even a cursory glance at the literature in the science of learning theory alerts us to a flagrant omission which, only gradually, is being corrected. I refer to what many epistemologists, in guarded and hushed tones, speak of as the human will. No one will deny there have been attempts to provide synonyms, substitute phraseology, all of which have fallen far short of their good intentions. These are the concepts of *motivation, spirit,* and even *drive.* The more sophisticated theorists have proven a little braver and used the word *psyche*, in spite of its many and differing connotations. Those taking this route have failed to sense the true potential inherent in the mind concept of will.

In the following pages I have defined will in relation to the cognitive and affective domains of the mind. What I have shown is that no learning takes place unless the mind experiences its subject or object. In essence, the mind must will to experience; only in this way does the mind find meaning. To experience, the mind must be fully functional, that is, there must be balance among its domains, namely, the cognitive, conative and affective. Otherwise, the mind is subject to the epistemological weakness of the rationalization process. In this process, the mind does not validate its values and, therefore, its learning is conditional. The apprehended knowledge is uncertain and remains as question.

Learning theory is an intriguing subject for discussion. To assist in the discussions I have included a number of simple case studies. In a sense, the material is all open-ended. This has been my intention. The approach will, I hope, stimulate considerable thought. If it does, I will have succeeded in my endeavor to bring before the learning theorist the need to seriously consider the place (therefore the task) of the will in human learning.

Russell A. Peterson

CHAPTER ONE

MENTAL BEHAVIOR

Behavior is a subject of intrigue for the epistemologist. It is exciting because of what he knows he must do with the concept. He is aware of his need to determine the functional relationship between mind and body, and perhaps even give the relationship a name, for instance, behavior. There is, however, another relationship which carries an even greater challenge, that is, the relationship of mind to itself. The particular dimension of this relationship which offers the greatest potential for analysis is the realization, by the mind, that it must use itself in order to analyze and know itself. This requires an understanding of its own behavior; we shall label it as mental behavior. It is on this construct we shall now concentrate.

In order to understand the type and depth of the problem which confronts us, it may be to our advantage to structure the presuppositions of mental behavior by means of questions. While the questions will be answered in the discussion of the subject, at this point they are being used to give us some idea of the size of the problem.

In a consideration of mental behavior, is it sufficient to say that such behavior is limited to what it is as an act, event or happening? If there is such a limitation upon mental behavior, does this exclude the mind from experiencing itself as the only means by which the mind is able to know? What is the relationship between cause and mental behavior? Is mental behavior always caused? If so, could one cause be psychological in nature? Does this imply the possibility that mental behavior could have its roots in what is physical to the exclusion of the mind? Or, are we willing to say that mental behavior is the reason for physical behavior? Or, is there a real difference between the two? If there is no difference between the two, is the connective consciousness? To what is consciousness committed? Can it be committed to anything else but to itself as mind? And, if it wishes to modify a relationship, is this modification process mental behavior? In mental behavior, are there presuppositions which literally demand constant modification because of what the mind experiences as a learner? Is this mental behavior modification the action which permits the mind to experience itself as mind? What does this tell the epistemologist about the mind in process of self-realization when the mind knows it must experience itself in order to learn? Does this not imply that the mind becomes its mental behavior when it experiences itself as its learning potential is actualized in what it comes to know? Is this the result of cognitive activity alone? To what degree is the conative held responsible as a determinant? If the affective domain in the intellective process has the opportunity for input, does this suggest that mental behavior may be affected by pure physical stimulation?

11

Or, does pure physical stimulation even exist? Or, is it possible for the act known as mental behavior to affect what is only physical? Does the 'only physical' even exist? Does mental behavior affect only the mind in complete isolation from what is purely physical? Does intentionality lodge itself in mind apart from mental behavior? Is it mental behavior which determines what mind intends? Is it what mind intends which can become what the body does? If so, what are the implications for the concept of cause in relation to what the body does? Is it possible for the body to do something which was not intended, by cause, in mind? What does this tell us about the nature of causality as a determinant apart from its relation to mind? Is the nature of the determinant changed when the mind assumes an active role and becomes self-determining? Are we under obligation then, to speak of mental behavior only when the mind is actively engaged in the learning process?

These are questions which confront us in our query about mental behavior. We shall start our search for answers in our consideration of the relationship between action and mental behavior.

1. Action and the Act

It seems strange that there exists the need to make such a statement as "even voluntary act can be traced back to causes . . . belonging to a world the agent never made." I am using these words only as a means to force to the surface another question, voluntary or involuntary, is there an act or movement which is not caused? Is there movement which does not possess causal antecedents? When we speak about reason for an act, are we not talking about the reason(s) in cause? Is there another way of justifying an act than by means of reason in cause, as this has become known and validated by mind before acting? The mind does not act isolated from its movement preceding the decision to act; nor, does it consider the act complete in itself, and as a finished product with nothing more to contribute to the further movement of the mind. An act is filled with motives; it is not an end in itself. It is done so the mind can move beyond its actions; it feeds, epistemologically speaking, upon its acts. The purpose is to make it possible for mind to move through its potentialities, those created by the movement which has become an act. The mind functions through its acts in order to function more effectively. The act is a presupposition in the movement we call the intellective process. To apprehend cause, the mind is in the process of knowing (coming to know) reason in cause; it is only in reason in cause that intention is found.

Look carefully at this example. It is my turn at home to dry the dishes. My wife is washing the dishes in the sink; I am at her side in charge of the towel. She hands me one of her most cherished plates and I drop it. The act is, dropping the plate. I did so involuntarily. I did not intend to do so. I, too, cherished the plate. Now, did cause have anything to do with, whether or not, the act was voluntary or involuntary? Why did I drop the plate? Because I was careless? Or, because my wife failed to rinse off the soap residue so the plate slipped from my fingers and became an accident? Or, knowing that perhaps there might be some soap remaining, I must take a firmer grip on the plate, but failed to do so? Or, because I had buried an anger, and even though I cherished the plate, to drop it would somehow compensate the cause of the anger? Could we summarize the conditions by saying that, whatever the reasons and their complexity, I dropped it because there was no way for me to hold on to it? The whole question of the accident will be treated elsewhere in the book, but can we not raise a number of questions with respect to the relationship between intention and the act at this point. For instance, if I was getting back at my wife, and even though the plate was slippery and I could have held on, I dropped it; the act was voluntary. I willed it. But, would I will it if the act was involuntary? Even in the case of accident? Now, new colors are appearing on the canvas. Intentionality is a characteristic of both the voluntary and involuntary act, with the exception of accident. I may intend, but does this say that even in the milieu of intention, will is apparent? Not at all. There are many things which I may intend to do, but which never get done. Is intention the criterion of responsibility or, is it the will? Is the concept of intention strong enough to bring us all the way to reason in cause?

Maybe I intended—quite unconsciously—to drop the plate because, secretly, I hate to dry the dishes, and to drop the favorite plate may be one way of losing the job.

Because the act was done does this mean the intention was realized, or completed? I willed to act, because the act was done. Or, did I? What is the criterion of responsibility here? Moreover, why bring in the idea of responsibility at this point in our discussion? What relevancy does it have for our thinking?

The plate was dropped (the act). Is the act something which can stand on its own feet? Or, is the act indicative of a responsibility which, in one sense, is not concerned with what has been done but, rather, why it was done, and what it is now causing the mind to do (by means of itself) in order to know the act and delineate it from its actions, those which proceeded and flowed from the act itself. In a sense, the mind now knows it must know the expressions of the act in order to determine the usefulness of the act and experience the complications of those expressions.

The mind is now forced to evaluate the implicative values inherent in an act and judge it according to the meaningfulness of the resultant movement.

The mind determines meaningfulness only as it has experienced the moral complicatives in the act itself. Without experiencing the act, the mind is confronted by nothing more than an event or happening, the relationship of which has not been experiential. When the mind experiences, it is in the process of decision, of making a value judgment, a moral verdict. It is answering the question, these are the reasons why I find meaning in the act, and for which (reasons) the act is done. The why is the question; the reasons the answers. Here is a procedure which insists that responsibility is an integral part of itself.

Responsibility

The question of determinism is pivotal in a discussion of the will and its relation to the learning process. Regardless of the brand carried by the learning strategist, he is aware that determinism is a problem because of the kinds of questions it raises about the nature, role, and purpose of the will. Seemingly, in learning theory, there are no two concepts more diametrically opposed to one another than will and determinism. And yet, the mind, in the process of learning, will never be understood until first the relationship between these two concepts has been delineated. One example of such a relationship is the psychological stance of the will in contending that determinism, because of its very nature, rather than relieving man of responsibility, thrusts upon him an even greater measure of accountability.

This is strange language to determinists. Well might it be. For, if it is true, many learning theorists will have to readjust their sights; the implications are many and cognitively severe. A study of the will must begin by defining relationships, the first of which is with determinism. But such a relationship cannot be defined without taking into consideration the place of responsibility given by the mind in the cognitive process. Therefore, we make our analysis of will by means of the doors open to us in the cognitive attribute responsibility.

Very simply, responsibility means, there is a rational agent. This means there has been an act, completed or in the process of completion. The mind is always concerned with action being done. There is, here, a relationship which has been formed between agent and action, one which carries a responsibility inherent in the sense of obligation. The agent is aware of his obligation, by means of the knowledge he possesses, to the choices present, and affected by his desicion which, ultimately, is actuated by an action.

The rational agent acts on knowledge which he has experienced and, therefore, found meaningful. As agent, because of this need to experience rationally, he recognizes that he must function as an autonomous being; the decisions he makes, the actions formed, are based wholly upon principles evolving from the relevatory knowledge which he alone possesses. It is a value judgment based upon predictives found in all value conditions. This means nothing more than the rational agent is a moral agent, and based upon purpose which is an integral part of every value (predictives are essential parts of purpose), depending upon the conditions which surround the actualization of the value, judgment is pronounced, and the value is appropriated for personal use. Here morality is seen as the bearer of responsibility by means of the conative principle.

Actually, it is as a moral agent that he is enabled to act (to bring about an action) as a rational agent. There is a point here with respect to the agent functioning as an autonomous being which needs clarification. The moral agent is fully free in his decisions, but this does not imply that he is the author of the moral principles by which his actions have been determined. Freedom which is found in rationality is not the autonomy of choice suggestive of such a thing as mere desire. The principles of morality lie outside the pale of a single mind. It is the single mind which is free to decide upon the efficacy of a particular moral principle, and determine whether or not it is meaningful to the extent that it will be allowed (willed) to effect a particular course of action. In such a decision it is the rational agent who puts into operation the moral principle, thereby making it possible for it to be effective, that is, a working cause. Thus, it is the rational agent who confronts us with the demand to determine the relationship between the moral principle and cause. The answer is to be found in his responsibility as a rational agent.

Rationalization (the power for) is a concept often subject to being played with by a mind unsure of its power for abstraction. To rationalize means to reason; are we always sure that the reasons which have been discovered are the correct ones?

And yet, its importance as a mind-factor must not be played down. The temptation to rationalize is always present in the mind. The process of rationalization is much like bias; the mind is aware of its need to know where it is at in relation to these factors at all times. Since the idea of the need to rationalize is fed from the unconscious, the mind knows it has an added responsibility, that of screening carefully the data fed to it by the processes of rationalization.

While it is the mind which rationalizes, it is also the mind which serves as its own self-corrective; one of the largest areas of responsibility lies in studying the many faces of rationalization. This is not to suggest that the mind is at odds with this ever-present activity; it simply demands to be in control of it. The mind, then, makes a distinction between the cognitive process and the processes of rationalization. It is rationalization which must be tested by the cognitive process and ultimately the entire intellective process, including the affective and conative. The unconscious is not safe ground for the mind until the consciousness of the self has declared it open for analysis.

There is a reason for whatever is done by the mind; until the mind cognizes its own reasons, the process remains but rationalization. In this way the mind understands its own intellective position; it is aware of the fact that quite often these reasons remain submerged in the unconscious, with perhaps but the tip above surface. It is possible for reason, then, to be only partially seen and little realized. It is the process of rationalization which is tempted to act on bits and pieces instead of upon the whole, as required by the intellective process.

When does one know one's reason for doing what has been done? There are two possibilities; the first, when the mind, quite passively, allows the unconscious and its reasons to suggest partial answers which are never questioned or analyzed for reliability or validity; the second, when the mind, quite actively, accepts the input from the unconscious, as well as from other sources, but subjects all reason to close intellective analysis and scrutiny. In the first instance, it is the mind functioning in its rational capacity and, in the second instance, in its totality as the intellective process.

The will begins to shift its cognitive gears when the mind has decided to accept its full responsibility for knowing when to move within the totality of its process. This it does only when it has determined the relevancy and value of the learning object. The will believes we can help doing what we do when we will to know; it is the will which continually insists upon the mind being actively engaged in the learning process; without this activity and cognitive determination, there is the temptation to settle for less than the ability to experience the object so meaning can be found.

This is the reason the will places as much emphasis upon belief as it does; it is important to know what we believe and why. If I say that I have the tendency to procrastinate, and I really don't know why I do it, this is simply to rationalize. Maybe the reasons why I procrastinate are buried in the unconscious and only suspicions are near the surface; the easy way out is to rationalize, perhaps even with false reasons. But the mind, acting *in toto*, is saying, I am going to force the unconscious to give up its secrets; this the mind, when it works by means of its intellective process, is able to do. Actually, it is the will speaking in loud tones saying, I believe it can be done, and what I believe must be known and used in further learning and understanding.

The intellect, in isolation, is unable to believe. In a sense, it is even ridiculous to suggest that it might possess this power. This would be the same as saying that to cognize is to have learned. But, there is the hint of another error as well; that is, to think that it is possible to possess an intellect in isolation. The intellect, as one of the functionaries of the mind, is but one integrator, which is able to function only because the affective and conative powers are also at work.

The intellect provides a setting of freedom in which the mind is able to function because of what it comes to believe. The mind is unable to believe without the freedom to believe. It is the intellect which provides the mind with options which must be analyzed and a decision made. The fact that the intellect functions through the options which are uncovered implies that the intellective process is well underway and the mind is drawing closer to a decision about what it can believe.

There is a morality, then, which determines the responsibility of the intellect in relation to belief. The source of that morality, while not decided by the will (but, indeed, motivated by it), lies in the teleological perspective of the given. To believe because of what is possible to find (or activate) in the given, and then to believe in the activated, because the evidence has been proven reliable and validated, is to determine the working perspective of the moral face present in the intellective process.

It is our belief that a moral sense exists in the intellective process. Its chief responsibility is to ask the question, why do you believe (in) that particular thing? Whenever the question why is asked, the moral face of the intellective process is staring at us. It is quite insistent that the question why, be answered, even to the point of suggesting that belief cannot exist without it. All of this is to the delight of the intellect. The question of why is the incentive, the cognitive push, needed by the intellect to begin to move. To ask why is to demand that some solid thinking is in order. The answer will never be found without it.

The subject of belief is one encountered at each step in the scientific method used in analysis. The mind recognizes the need to believe before the next step is taken. Unless this premise is accepted and followed, ignorance will be added to ignorance, and the size of the mountain of uncertainty will grow.

Of course, it is true that the belief formulated may be but a matter of hypothesis; this is the chief characteristic of belief; it makes itself constantly available for test purposes. The object of belief does not want to be believed unless its existence can be proven. The mind wills to believe only what has been proven certain and true.

This presents another problem for the intellect. We have said thinking must take place. The mind knows what thinking is because it must do the thinking; this is not the problem. The problem is, what factors engendered by the principles underlying the relationships between essences in the problem itself affect the intellective process? It is time we realize that the intellective process and the thought process are one and the same.

Unless the thought process is aware of the cognitive implications of the factors suggested above, the freedom to believe will not exist. The mind insists that its functionaries are in total command of the necessities for learning. Here, again, the moral influence is being felt by the intellect. What is actually being said by the mind to the intellect is: you must be in full command of your thought processes; it is what we believe and why which is important, not what the object of our hypothetical belief wants us to believe.

The mind believes that it is possible to know; when it does come to know, it wants to know what it can believe. The mind is now taking into consideration the affective dimension of its responsibility; it knows that what it believes has a profound influence upon the choices it makes. The active mind wants to know what is done for reasons inherent in its beliefs, and not for the untested subjectivities often present in the affective realm. The affective, much like the rational desire, often tries to move without taking with it the cognitive and conative domains.

If we wish, we may speak of belief as a pre-condition of all knowledge; that is, knowledge gained by experiencing an object, thereby actualizing meaning. Such a proposition suggests a number of dangers, the greatest of which is the question, what is the source of belief? Is it something without benefit of the intellective process? These questions are answered by one of the above statements; the mind wants to know what it can believe and why. It is a pre-condition of knowledge. A paradox? Not at all.

Belief, for the intellective process, is the self-correcting factor inherent in every existent. I believe (posit) so that I can know what to believe and why. Belief, in this sense, as the pre-condition, is the working hypothesis of every existent. Learning takes place in the presence of a problem; the problem exists because there is the belief of an existent.

To believe is also a process; one believes in order to believe. Belief insists that it be given the opportunity to correct what it believes, if necessary. In this way belief feeds on belief. Without it, the mind cannot function.

Because it is self-corrective, it insists that it can function only when the mind *in toto* is free, that is, free to change its own mind. Belief, as a pre-condition to knowledge, is the means by which the mind keeps open the doors between its tendency toward passivity and the demand for movement and activity. Belief in the potentiality of every existent is what keeps the mind from settling for the results of rationalization.

To rationalize, the passive mind is explaining to itself, on the basis of incomplete data, what only seems reasonable. There is a dependency upon a probability inadmissable to the intellective process. Very often reason for the process of rationalization is quite different than reason for the affective, cognitive and conative processes. There is an incompleteness in rationalizing which leaves the intellective process epistemologically uncomfortable. This uncomfortable feeling is due to the belief that the rationalizing mind has not concerned itself with cause, as it should. There is even some question whether in the process of rationalization, the mind is aware of the causal characteristic, let alone the conditions of cause and its reason for existence. Moreover, there is considerable question whether the process of rationalization increases the freedom of the mind as the intellective process insists upon doing. The source of suspicion lies in this: since rationalization is a product (developmental in nature) of the passive components of the mind, there is, perhaps, the tendency to be manipulated by the object; that is, the mind in this instance is epistemologically affected by data (incompletely known) and decisions are reached which are incorrect. The empirical controls evident in the intellective process are seldom found in the rationalization process. The intellective process knows what to do with data; when this is not true for the rationalization process, the incomplete and uncontrolled and unanalyzed is free to manipulate and control the process. The tip of the floating iceberg often deceives with respect to its true size.

What the intellective process is saying then, about the rationalization process, is this. The rationalization process is not to be trusted until its components of mind become active; but then, when this happens, it loses its characteristics and becomes the intellective process. The intellective process bespeaks a high sense of empirical responsibility, controlling the effect of facts and their implications, rather than allowing facts to control the mind. To control the effect of a fact is to dissect its essence until it is rendered transparent and, thus, known. Only then is the mind able to judge and determine the meaning of meaning. Only then has the mind experienced the true potentiality of a fact, and determined its relevancy for application. This is choice, but it is also the mind in movement as it acts to know.

Rationalization often deceives; not that this is its purpose, but because it shrinks from knowing in terms of completeness. Rationalization suffers from the epistemological disease known as illusion; there is a readiness to accept the hypothesis as knowledge. The disease of illusion tends to work on this premise: to explain away is the same as the tested explanation, the cornerstone of the intellective process.

Does all of this demand the need for determinism? Does determinism carry a logic within itself which says, as the mind is determined, it must determine if it is to function according to the purpose of its nature?

But a question of a more serious nature is this one, does determinism take from the mind all sense of responsibility? This question brings us to our second statement about responsibility. The first point was the recognition that responsibility means there is a rational agent. To this we now add, as a rational agent, he must be aware of those implications which describe and affect the relationship between determinism and responsibility; such a relationship forces him to possess a working definition of both concepts, determinism and responsibility. Moreover, it forces him to analyze his own psychological movements, and come to some conclusion about the relevancy of those movements (accountability) and the degree of experiencing taking place.

The whole idea of responsibility is one which never escapes the concern of will. Because of its concern, it has, as one example, defined responsibility knowing, however, that perhaps its definition may be quite different from the way the rationalization process defines it.

Will thinks in terms of movement; for will, act is movement because act is never completed; it is in process because the implications of act make it a dynamic construct, imprinting its implication upon someone or something. Thus, the will is insistent that the learner is responsible for all movement which evolves from him as person. This is a basic and unretractable premise. The assumption underlying the premise is a clear one, concise and significant for our thinking. While the learner may be subject to determinants, external or internal in nature, it is intellective stance (the total intellective process) which governs whether or not he will allow himself to be determined, or will exert his intellectual and willful powers of self-determination. It is our contention that responsibility, as we are using it here, is rightfully assumed only when the powers of self-determination are exercised. This is seen in the kinds of questions the will persists in asking in reference to movement by the learner.

The will asks: when is the learner accepting the need to be responsible so that he can experience the object? Even the word 'when' speaks of process. The answer, the learner is responsible when he is in the process of determining the 'why' of movement. This, of course, addresses itself to the question of cause; cause is interested in explanation, but explanation is sterile without an understanding of how the why is justified. Here the mind speaks of conditions and reasons; here the will concerns itself with the developmental prerogatives of value and its implicative intentions. To be able to answer these questions, a particular quality of responsibility is needed.

The learner is accountable for movement, what he does, in the way he does it, and the reasons for which he does it. Movement evolves from a mind actively engaged in meeting the determinants inherent in every confrontation.

The reason why the will is concerned at this point, in addition to what has been said above, is this. The degree of responsibility will be in keeping with the degree of awareness found in the consciousness of the learner. How conscious is he of his responsibility as a self-determiner? Without this consciousness, the will will realize that the mind subjects itself to determinants which may assume all responsibility for what is done.

The will insists that it be allowed to become the determiner that the procession inherent in movement be governed by a high degree of consciousness, the degree determined by the point at which responsibility is accepted.

It is responsibility which believes that all dimensions of movement possess, as its essence, a moral nature. This means that just as it is necessary for the learner to define determinism and responsibility and the nature of their relationship, so it is necessary for him to be aware of the moral implications of movement. To know the moral implications of the act is to accept the responsibility inherent in intention; what is intended implies purpose; all purpose is contingent upon a moral base. As a self-determiner, result is intended even though it is recognized that often accident will cause movement to actualize a resultant different from the intention. In both cases, cause was at work; the intention remains a validated moral construct. When the result is as intended, he doesn't have far to go to find the reasons for justification of movement; justification must be seen as an integral part of intention. To intend is to justify movement for reasons validated in cause. This line of argument permits us to again assert a basic premise: to be consciously responsible (there is no unconscious responsibility) is to be morally responsible for an act which continues as movement.

When the learner wills, as well as the what of his willing, he is responsible for what he wills, whenever it is done. As a self-determiner, he knows he cannot use the old excuse of the mind which has been determined (because it wanted to be determined); cause made him do it. The determined mind is not the responsible mind.

The learner finds his freedom of mind only in the degree of responsibility he assumes in the learning process. Freedom and its degrees are always in relation to cause. The incentive for movement by mind lies in the reasons in cause as these remain open to become known. Closed reasons in cause lead to a mind determined and therefore ignorant (unlearned).

The mind which generates epistemological energy refuses to look upon cause as an entity or as something living only in the past. The mind generating movement brings all existents, especially cause, to a contemporary and volitile status. Cause is not something which is completed (as an act) nor can its movement be brought to a stop. The prime responsibility of cause is to cause, its energy directed to the never finished product, the human mind. It is the self-determining mind (the responsible mind) which brings the reasons in cause to the on-going activity of ceaseless movement. What cause brings into being is the mind in the process of causing. It is cause which realizes itself through the activity and movement of the mind; it is cause and its reasons which provide the mind with the opportunities upon which to move in its knowing quest.

Freedom of will, in its relation to responsibility, lies within its responsible ability to do or not do. A moral commitment evidenced in intention determines the parameters in which the learner desires to move. He can do otherwise, but not intentionally. He has the ability to do otherwise, but not to act responsibly and move in the direction he wills. He wills in freedom, and for the freedom to be found in chosen areas of responsibility. The "idea" of 'can' is governed either by the persistency of a cause seeking only to deter- mine, or by a mind responsible enough to itself to take from cause and its reasons what it (mind) can generate, when so directed. Is there an absolute about the idea of can? Nor, is cause an absolute; the nature of its uncertainty rests with the decision of the mind. It is mind and its intentions which can change, so quickly, the role of cause. There is a freedom which is necessary for the learner to possess in order to be morally responsible for his intellective movements.

Intention

The question which now confronts us is this, am I always aware of what I am doing? At this point in the question there are two concepts which command our attention: (1) the word aware, and (2) the word doing. Since awareness implies consciousness, this relationship raises a host of other questions. Doing implies activity, and the implication, then, is evident. We must now expand the question to read, If I am aware of my activities, is it possible for this awareness to direct those same activities in order to actualize what was originally intended in the action? The emphasis now shifts to the word intention. It is a word which may not be as nebulous as it appears.

First, let us say, by way of introduction, that it is impossible to analyze this concept without taking into consideration the implications of awareness and action by way of their relationship to intention.

To emphasize the logic of our argument, we proceed slowly and schematize each step.

1. Action. I am writing this book. Moreover, I know I am in the process of writing it.

2. Knowledge. Because I know I am writing it, the specificity of the action is very clear. I can explain and thus describe each step necessary in completing the action as process.

3. Predictability. Because of the length of the process, and what is involved (research and writing), it is possible to predict, unless conditions make it impossible, that I shall continue to research and write tomorrow and even for the next year.

Before we analyze each of these steps, there is a persistent knock at our epistemological door. The question is asked, Wherein lies the intention? It would be a simple matter if we could limit our answer to saying, There would be no action such as writing the book unless I had intended to write it, as well as decided to do the research and thinking necessary to prepare the self for writing it. All of this is true. This is one of our assumptions. However, is intention an integral part of action? Our answer is, Yes. I am writing this book. I am writing it as I planned (intended) to write it, with minor changes. Moreover, I know that I am writing it as I intended, always leaving a margin for change.

Because I know I am writing it, the specificity of the action is clear. Why? Because I am acting upon the preparation and decisions already made in the original intention. Here is the clearest example of what we mean by the actualization of intention in action. I can explain what I am doing, because what I am doing is the actualization of intention. My intentions reach to the futurity dimension as well. I intend to be writing six months from now.

Taking into consideration my teaching and administrative duties, the time this leaves me for writing, and knowing the number of pages it is possible to write each day, my daily writing activities are governed by what I intend to cover in this book, as well as the conditions already listed. One intention is to finish the writing of the book, but to do so means fulfilling all of the obligations related to its actual writing.

Thus, it is readily apparent there are a number of operational points in reference to intention and its decisions. While the original intention was to write this book, action was intended, for one thing, because of the inherent potentialities at many points along the way.

There is a spin-off here we must think about for a moment. It deals with my knowledge of what I am now doing, and, what I intend to do six months from now. Is my knowledge of present action predicated on a past action? Certainly. I decided to write the book four years ago. Why did I decide to write it? Because of the encouragement of colleagues? In part. Because I had completed the research? In part. Primarily, however, because I have now reached the place in my own intellectual pilgrimage where I feel ready to write it. This means I have found enough evidence in my research methodology, thought processes and writing ability to imply, if you decide to write it, you have everything going for you. Since I now have this assurance, I intend to write a carefully researched book. My intention, based on what I am convinced is empirical data, is to actualize the intention so carefully prepared. Ability to perceive the implications of an intention fostered identifications; it was a carefully validated criteria which heeded the potentiality for realization.

It is important that we carefully define this relationship.

1. A moment ago I opened the window near my writing desk. We may now ask the question, Did I intentionally open the window? Yes. Why? Because it is too warm and stuffy in the vicinity of my desk. Now before I arrived at the desk, I did not intend to open the window, with the exception, however, of this thought. Whenever the conditions described above exist when I arrive at my desk, I open the window. In one sense, there is a built-in potentiality here, unless, there are new conditions, such as, this morning I may have a cold, and to follow my regular procedure may aggravate it; so, in spite of any habitual intention, I do not open the window.

2. From this basic assumption arises another thought question. If the identical conditions exist tomorrow when I arrive, do I now intend to open the window? Again, the answer is, Yes. I intend to open the window whenever the conditions warrant it. The significance of the conditions is one which the mind does not by-pass in the movement of the intellective process.

3. If there is no question about the relationship between intentionality and futurity, what about the past as a referrent? Nothing is changed in the argument. A few years ago I fully intended to spend a few months of intensive

study at the Hebrew University in Jerusalem. Permission had been granted for the study by University officials, plane reservations were made, but the conditions of war made my stay impossible.

We summarize these points before we move on in our discussion. It is well to note a number of characteristics of the decisions connected with intentionality, the first of which is the place of the thought process in the decision. Intentionality is a mind-set, the implications of which are determined by validated conditions. This means that in each case cited above, my decision was psychologically verbalized; ideas were generated, alternatives considered, and, at all times, I knew what I meant as I used thoughts to express my intention. There is a directness about intentionality because I am aware of implied meaning.

If we wish to pursue this, there is a second characteristic which is important to our thinking, but does not change or detract from our original premises. The conditions are present and purpose is evident. After my morning lecture on the subject of existentialism, I listed three books which I intend the members of the class to read before the next lecture; only by doing this reading will they be enabled to follow the arguments presented in the lecture.

From what has been implied in the above paragraphs, there are a number of conclusions which can be drawn.

1. We posit the premise that all action is intended, consciously or unconsciously. This premise is based, in turn, on the belief that whatever is done, is done so something else can be completed or achieved. I lift my foot in order to place it on the step; I raise my arm to remove a picture from the wall, because I intended to walk up to that particular step and, to take the picture from the wall. On the other hand, even though I may not consciously intend, at this time, to attend the symphony concert this evening, conditions may change, and I may decide to attend, after first deciding not to. Intention often is habitual in the sense that I do not cognize action by analyzing intentions, such as knowing that if I wish to cross campus, as I intend to do, I shall walk; I know there is no other way of crossing unless someone carries me, which is quite out of the question at the moment. This is what has been called a "fulfilled presumption." But, even this argument does not detract from our premise. Even in presumption there is intentionality.

2. The conclusion arrived at above frees us to linger for a moment over an epistemological left-over. This lingering will lead us to a second conclusion. Intentionality moves from an empirical base; what is the empirical base from which unintentionality moves? We stated that all action is intended. Is it possible then, to speak of an unintended action? Are there conditions under which the self does something which was not intended? Some years ago I witnessed an accident in which a student was injured. He was standing on the

edge of the roadway waiting for a car to pass. Evidently he was standing on a piece of ice; as the car was passing, the student shifted his standing position, slipped and fell into the side of the automobile.

The student had no intention of being injured. There was action, without intentionality.

We must dispose of this example quickly; however, it enables us to use the accident describing a condition which is external to what the mind of the student had already decided. The student had decided to wait until the car passed before crossing the street in order not to be injured. Moreover, we can safely assume that he was not aware of the ice patch under his feet; if he was, he did not realize the potential danger; if he did, he did not exercise proper caution; regardless of these "ifs" he did not intend to be thrown into the side of the passing car.

Our conclusion is this. Intention is a mind-action, and pure accident, while there is always cause, is usually not intended; if one intends an accident it is no longer an accident.

In describing the relationship between intention and action, it is well to keep in mind that if the action is by accident or, a mistake, we must be careful of our usage of the term intentionality. Or, might we more properly ask, Under such conditions is the term even applicable? Moreover, is the term applicable in the relationship between intent and intentionality? Are they two different terms? Are we suggesting there is a difference even if we see one as a verb and the other as a noun? We raise these questions because epistemologists have been known to suggest that intentionality is the same as action itself, that is, as doing something.

The distinction must be kept clear; while intentionality may be a noun and refer to a specific action, the nature of purpose is always verb-ish. Intentionality does not do. Rather, it is what the mind works with, as an intimate part of the intellective process which moves the physical (or mental) component to act.

The statement, "It is what the mind works with" is an interesting one, worthy of further thought. While we discuss the epistemological premises of the mind in many places in this study, our context feeds us with an unanswered question. Do I always know what I am doing? If so, does this knowledge assure me that what I am doing is the result of intentionality?

What does the mind work with? A partial answer is, intentions. Before we move on, we return to the first question, do I always know what I am doing? Hints as to the answer have been already given. A friend who has been in a serious accident is under heavy sedation. He raises his arm and strikes it against the side of the bed. He is unaware of what he has done. In other words, he was not conscious of what he did. Nor, was I, when months ago, my arm slipped from the side of the chair and struck a low table. I was conscious at all times, but I did not intend the arm to fall. However, I was not aware of the close proximity of the arm to the edge; my consciousness was not directed at a specificity. I was intent upon my writing. I knew what I was doing, namely, writing, but I did not know the whereabouts of the arm in an empirical sense. A directed consciousness is an important factor to take into consideration when looking at the nature of intention.

What does the mind work with? Another partial answer is, the logicality which is the intention.

This, of course, speaks to the question of cause. Our question now becomes, Is intention the cause of an action? Or, is intention the means by which the mind decides to act? If we wish, we may turn to the suggestion of description for our answer, such as "intentions cannot be said to be causes of action, place; in principle, no description of an intention can be given which is independent of the description of the action which is said to be its effect." Now, while we, too, believe that intentions cannot be causes of action, the explanation of description and its relevancy leaves something to be desired.

We return to an early example. I intend to walk across the campus. To describe the intention and relate it to cause and suggest that because I intend to make the walk and therefore cause myself to actually do it, is to forget that intention is a confrontation, a psychological directive stance which stands before the mind in a relationship demanding reaction before an action takes place. I intend to cross campus. If I actually do, it is another matter. The mind is now reacting to the suggestion which is intention. I intend to cross campus to mail a letter. Since there is no other way to mail the letter but to cross campus, the suggestion for fulfillment of a decision (to mail the letter) is inherent as intention, namely, I intend to cross campus because I intend to mail the letter. Here is cause, when I act. On the other hand, I intend to cross campus to mail the letter, but I am tired and so I decide not to make the walk. What about cause in this circumstance? Is there action unless I will to act on intention? Is not the real cause of my crossing campus, the doing of my intention? Unless I willed to act, intentions remain meaningless and motionless.

There are arguments to suggest "that no independent description of the intention can be given (which) is to say that there is an internal connexion between the concepts of intention and related action." Certainly there is an "internal connection" between the concept of intention and related action, but this connection is not predicated on the idea of description. Rather, it is predicated on the concept of will which causes the intention to become actualized. This mind action alone determines the nature of the internal connection. And, while we, too, can quote Hume by saying that the causal connection is a contingent one, and we agree, although we are extracting from a special context the idea, it is only the idea with which we are concerned at the moment. The causal connection between intention and action is a contingent one because of the fact the will may decide to be passive or determined and not exert its rightful role of determining the nature of cause. I intend to walk across campus because I intend to mail a letter, but I am unmotivated to do so. So, I don't make the walk. The will is passive; it doesn't really care; in a weak sense it wills not to will and become a cause of action, the cause of inaction. Intention had its object, but mind-action cancelled mind-action. The will is a powerful force; it is dealing with itself and this is where so many of its difficulties lie. What does happen in the mind when it is in the process of "forming" intentions?

The first thing to remember is that intention is not mind. Intention is a resultant of the intellective process. It is the mind which intends; thus, in a sense, it is the sum total of the operation of the mind at a given moment. Moreover, because it is a resultant of the intellective process, and reason is the functional base from which the intellective process moves, intention possesses a logic, the logic of cause in the intellective process.

This is our first cue about how the mind forms an intention. It is brought into being by means of the intellective process. Secondly, there is a logic in what the mind intends.

It is my intention to cross campus; Why do I intend to make this move? To post an over-due letter. Thus, I intend to cross campus for a logical reason. The relationship is quite evident. My only reason for crossing campus is to post the letter.

We must be careful, not to jump to conclusions too rapidly. For instance, I intend to cross campus because I intend to post a letter. Well and good. But, this does not tell me how the mind, by means of the intellective process, actually wills the formation of the intention.

We use the same example. One part of my intention in crossing campus and posting the letter is related to a personal concern. The person to whom the letter is being sent, in two days is leaving for Europe. Unless it is posted this morning he will not receive it. It is of greatest importance that it is received before he arrives in Europe. Here is our contingency factor, as well as another dimension to the logic of which we spoke above. To post the letter is but a means to fulfill an intention that is based on a condition revealed in the movement of the intellective process, a movement, in turn, based on the logic inherent in a contingency. When there is a logical intent it means the mind has weighed, by its processes, all contingencies, made a decision and is now ready to will action.

It now becomes quite evident the mind is working as a self-determiner. It is because it is necessary for the letter to be delivered within two days (because of its importance) that I cross the campus and post the letter, rather than remaining at my desk and continuing to write.

The will has picked up the logic in the reason for movement, validated the need, and literally picked me up from my chair and forced me into action.

There has been a validation process, *a priori*-wise, for intention; if this were not true, I would wait until after my assigned writing time to post the letter because the time element would not have been the important factor in itself.

2. Act and Cause

As seen in the preceeding pages, it has been our contention that where act is, cause exists. This purpose is an important one because of our belief that cause serves as the phenomenological energizer for the learning process. Moreover, it is our contention that no real learning takes place unless the mind, by means of the intellective process, has experienced cause. This means five things: first, cause is recognized by means of its reason for existence; second, in reason lies the logic of purpose and design; what exists reflects the teleological principles inherent in the reason(s) in cause; third, in these reasons lie the motive for their own existence, as well as provides the motive for the mind to experience their essence; fourth, in motive lies the value which can 'become' for the mind; fifth, when value and motive are seen as purpose, the intention of cause has been revealed and seen as the source of the potentiality in cause. It is only at this point in the learning process that the mind wills to act. Without this experiencing act what happens is but a happening, an event without an epistemological base.

The Causal Law

These five premises force us to ask this question, What is causal law, and what is its relationship to act?

The moment we speak of causal law, does this not imply a determinism (almost a compulsion) which takes from the mind the freedom to choose and therefore the impossibility of becoming a self-determiner? My answer, of course, must be in the negative. These are my reasons. When I use the idea of causal law, I am saying there is a universal causality which I am free to suggest exists because of this premise: what exists has a cause, and whatever exists is universal in nature. Whatever exists has been created, therefore caused. This logic permits me to posit the existence of First Cause as The Mind which brings all things into existence. There is reason in First Cause, the logic realized, by the created, in the design and form, the nature, scope and purpose, of what has been caused. The basal axiom of reason in Cause is the implanted reason(s) in what has been caused, the opportunities for knowing essence. The animate, the human, is what I am talking about here, the created human, the learner, caused but with the phenomenological energy to, in turn, cause. Out of the Mind of First Cause the existent evolved and became mind. The potentiality of this mind lies in what is universal, the causal law which has as its purpose, the enabling of mind to 'become' by means of the reason(s) at its disposal. Here is an act in the process of being completed because of its freedom to will the meaning of its own existence.

Consciousness

All of which requires the recognition that mind is consciousness. It is consciousness and its essence which reminds us of the real responsibility of the mind in relation to act, namely, the need to conceptualize the potential inherent in act itself. By means of the process of conceptualization, the mind becomes aware of the meaning of the act through its potentialities, in a sense, through the perspective of its being.

Act is not an isolated entity, something which the mind does, nor is it the thing which happens as a result of a decision by the mind; rather, it is an extension as movement of mind actualizing intention by means of its object.

The Free Act?

If there is to be movement, the mind must be free. And this means?

First, it is not the act which is free, but rather, the mind.

Second, it is the mind which must be free if it is to function experientially, that is, psychologically, the only way in which we can speak about freedom in relation to mind, and do so, recognizing the limitations of what we call the causally effective. It is the reason in cause which allows me to hold this pen; I am free to do so because of what (causally) the pen is; I am not free (causally) to lift the desk at which I am writing. In this latter case, there is no act, and the mind sees no need to justify even the need to try (act) and lift the desk, since it already has conceptualized the problem and concluded that because of size and weight, it is an impossibility.

It is not the act and its possibilities, which must be free, then, but the mind in order for it to function experientially. It is G. E. Moore who makes the conjunctive 'if' pivotal in this connection. He tells us we are free to do an act if we can do it if we want to; that which we can do if we want to is what we are free to do. Again, we raise the question, is there freedom when conditions are attached? The conditions may look like this. Moore says we can do an act if we can do it; I can't lift the desk, so, I can't do it—even though I want to. Wanting to do something, of course, is not enough to posit the statement: that which we can do if we want to is what we are free to do. I am not free to lift the desk, to do the act. What does this do for our argument? Nothing. The argument doesn't even touch on our points of question. Freedom is in relation to mind and what it knows can and cannot be done; it knows from the reasons in that which is causally effective.

Freedom exists only in relation to the mind-act and the movement known as action. I am free to lift my arms; the man across the room who is sitting on his hands is not free to lift his arms. Here are conditions, the nature of which are determined by factors which may or may not be mind-acts. The man sitting on his hands may have decided to do this to keep himself from lifting his arms. Now, again, we move into another realm of epistemological speculation. I am free to lift my arms, but he is not. Why? The mind becomes very much interested at this point, but it eased into the problem much earlier, for instance, at the time the man decided to sit on his hands because, if he lifted them, he might be asking for permission to speak, which he does not want to do and he knows this is the only way to keep himself under control. The power confrontation always lies in the decision-making function and prerogative of the mind. It is for this reason the mind must be kept free, rather than the act. The act is a free one only when the mind has been free to make the act free.

The mind is free when it is conscious of the potentialities of its freedom. This means also that it is aware of the presence of those slim fingers of the unconscious that are constantly reaching out to force their way into the conscious, and have their psychological affect upon the knowledge of consciousness. Consciousness, using the totality of its mind's processes, knows when it knows, and when it can act, and when it is unable to act. To recognize ability is to recognize potentiality as well as limitations, and what it possesses, or does not possess, in order to act. This is mind-movement, mind action. It wills to act because it is free to do—within what it knows can be causally effective. Freedom is dependent upon the knowledge possessed about the reasons in cause; it is governed by the logic of the design in reason, and the limitations which are imposed by means of the potentiality determined.

Here is an active mind at work, epistemologically speaking.

The Free Act? With Conditions.

If we were willing to admit the existence of such a thing as a free act (which we are not), the question which follows would be in keeping with the premise: does the free act proceed causally from an act of choice? Is it not a question of the freedom of choice rather than the freedom of the act? Conditions which make it necessary, or possible, for the mind to function relate to the reason in cause and ultimately affect choice; act is not the mover, rather, it is the essence of movement; the mover needs the freedom to move and bring movement into being; movement becomes act in the process of becoming. It is choice which is caused before act is free to come into being. This is the only sense in which we can call an act free. The criteria related to choice must first be met before act is caused.

This, however, does not answer the problem question about the relation between condition and act, freedom and choice. The proposition above was suggested to permit us to taste more completely certain epistemological delights, such as, in choice, what characteristic of mind must be present if the mind is to function freely? The answer, It must be able to bring to the surface of consciousness those empirical data which make it possible to choose and act because the mind is satisfied that such action will be of value. The empirical data are the conditions which make me free to act freely. An example. I am standing on the shore of a lake. I hear a call for help and see a young man struggling to keep afloat. I am now confronted with a choice and the need to act. How I act is dependent upon the choice I make. If I am impulsive (not responsible) I might jump in and try and save the life of the boy. But, if I jump in—knowing I can't swim? Or, I weigh the conditions of the problem such as, distance, my own ability as a swimmer, existing strength, speed necessary to reach him in time; if I am unable to meet these conditions, the chances are very great that I, too, will drown. Or, perhaps there is another alternative such as a boat, knowing that I can row faster than I can swim. What I do is dependent upon what I choose and why. Why I choose what I do is dependent upon the logic (empirical data) available to me as I make the choice. Here is mind acting responsibly because it is depending upon the moral ingredient inherent in the reasons in cause. What is moral in jumping in for the rescue when I am not able to swim, and the distance and time problem make it impossible to reach him in time? The criteria inherent in conditions carry a morality which strives to keep the mind from becoming compulsive in nature; the self-determining mind acts responsibly; its consciousness is aware of the implications of the conditions in cause; it knows it cannot afford to become compulsive. The mind acts responsibly when there is no reason to question the choice; herein it validates its action: there was absolutely no way for me to reach the drowning man in time. I could not act freely.

Now, however, if I so much as doubted my ability to reach him, but held to the possibility that it could be done, we face a different kind of problem. The conditions tell me that the chance is slight, but—. The value which I now place upon the possibility becomes my concern, and the cause leading to choice. At no time have I not valued the saving of the life of the young man. Now, in this case, my decision is: any chance is worth (my value) taking. Again, the mind is not acting compulsively but, rather, by surfacing the empirical base of my value system. I now become in even greater measure, a self-determiner. I have examined the conditions leading to chance and now will to act.

It is in choice that the mind makes known its intention; the actualization of intention is the act. While the intention is a future projection, it is the act which brings into the present the actualization of the reasons in intention.

The mind is aware of a problem here, however. It is fully cognizant of one of its own weaknesses, namely, the often spineless quality of intention, that is, the weakness which is always present, of allowing itself to be determined. When intention remains only intention, the mind is a thing determined. I might have every intention of trying to save the drowning boy but, even though the data tells me all systems are green, I don't enter the water.

What is missing? The will to act. Why is there no will to act? Because I don't want to. What kind of a reason is that? It might be lethargy. Even that is a reason.

There is always a reason why we act or don't act. If there is a reason, there is a cause for that reason; it may not be rational but it is still a reason. And, we rationalize it, even when our intention was good, and correct. Intention, then, is not a prediction suggesting that it is an absolute. Even at the stage of intention, the mind recognizes its need to intellectualize the process and bring intention to actualization. Of course the mind is free to change its mind, but in so doing it still must answer the question, Why? To change its own mind also requires the will to act, and this it does not do until it has valued its reasons.

The relationship between intention and responsibility is an intriguing one; one not to be considered lightly by the epistemologist. Intention and responsibility have characteristics which suggest the need to probe deeply into their nature. Perhaps we can best get at their nature by raising certain questions.

First, with respect to intention. Here we wish to raise the question, Does such a thing as an intentional act actually exist? Rather, do we not mean that it is the mind which acts on its intention, and the act itself is not intentional? Intention refers to mind, not to the act. This forces us to look at intention in a way that its relationship to responsibility cannot be ignored. The self-determined mind is responsible for the decisions which become intentions, and ultimately for their actualization. Is there an example when the mind is not responsible for its intention? No. Here is the reason.

The example of vicarious responsibility is often cited. The case of a man responsible for wrongful acts committed say, by one's agent, "acts which no intention of his could have prevented," is a good one. But it says nothing to our problem, since it is our contention that vicarious responsibility is a figment of an over-stressed mind. Intention is an extremely personal thing; I cannot be held vicariously responsible for the intent of someone else; I can however, be held vicariously responsible for the act of someone else such as my agent.

Second, with respect to responsibility. Responsibility is to the intent, not to the act. We become responsible to our own act while it is in the process of actualizing itself, to the degree that it becomes self-correcting. This involves intention; intention describes the degree of responsibility I have assumed toward the object of my intentions. The cycle is a short one, in many ways. I intended to submit my grades to the Registrar's Office on time, but it wasn't done. Why? The answer to this question will describe the degree of responsibility which I did or did not assume. What we have here is a very human problem.

The Human Act

We inject this idea because of its importance to a consideration of intent and responsibility. We call the act human because it is the human mind in action, and not something done by an external to the mind. Moreover, because it is human action, as human it is subject to the intellective weaknesses of its own being. It is because of its humanness that the act becomes the result of a mind which has been determined, or the mind which is a self-determiner. The prime characteristic of the self-determined mind is its spontaneity of action. It is spontaneous in its activity because of its freedom; while it recognizes the presence of conditions, it is by means of those conditions (and their inherent reasons for existence) that they are enabled to move. The moving mind is the spontaneous mind; the movement is propelled by the empirical deliberations of the intellective process. It is spontaneity which receives its impetus from the purposive momentum of intent, the means by which the deliberations ensure the process of adequate emphasis on method as well as on ends. We are now saying that choice is always deliberative; the particular act which literally actualizes the choice speaks to the act as being voluntary or involuntary, while, in reality, it is to choice and the means by which the mind conceptualizes the process of choice that the question of voluntary/involuntary applies.

The Voluntary Act?

While we do not believe that it is the act which is free, but, rather, the mind, the same typology of structure can be applied to the voluntary act. Act is a resultant, a part of movement; it is the mind which voluntarily or involuntarily acts. This contention must be kept in mind as we proceed to develop our argument.

The mind voluntarily acts when it is conscious of doing so; this means, when it is aware of the fact of what is being done. This is true for the mind which is determined by epistemologically oriented environmental circumstances, or the mind which has attained the status of a self-determiner. In the first instance, the mind may or may not know in a lesser degree what is going to happen because there is an attitude of empirical resignation about it; in a sense, it doesn't care. It has already made up its mind that it cannot, or will not, do anything about what is happening. To do even this, requires a degree of consciousness and awareness. For the self-determined mind, however, it voluntarily does and consequently acts because of the high degree of awareness, i.e., knowledge which it possesses about the reasons or cause. It is the degree of consciousness which tightens the relationship to cause; the mind moves to act because its knowledge (experientially gained) assures it that it is epistemologically feasible to do so; it now moves voluntarily.

What the mind knows with certainty is a fact; it is a fact because the mind has experienced its essence and determined its meaning; upon these suppositions mind is then free to act; if it wills to act, it does so voluntarily. The intensity of the relationship is reached when the mind wills, and there is the movement which indicates an act is in the process of completing the designed intention.

The reality of the degree of consciousness is the source of momentum. The degree of consciousness is governed by the degree of intensity evidenced in the relationship between mind and cause. While in one way the reasons in cause remain passive, awaiting the decision of mind to probe its meaning, it is the degree of the desire to know which activates mind to will. The greater the consciousness of potentiality, the greater the potentiality of the mind reaching the point of becoming willing to act. There is a delicate balance in this nuance; we must be careful not to underrate its importance in the intellective process. Nor, must we fall into the learning trap by believing that it is consciousness which may deceive the mind at this point; if the mind is deceived, it is because it is not functioning on its true empirical level of analysis.

An act, then, which has been willed according to the logic inherent in the methodology of the self-determined mind, is voluntary because of the spontaneity engendered by means of the reasons in cause. The mind thinks by means of its methodology. The whole idea of deliberation is an important one because of its responsible relationship to choice. Deliberation is a characteristic of the self-determined mind, one which acts voluntarily because it now knows the value of acting toward a profitable and acceptable end.

It is this responsible relationship which I believe Thomas Aquinas was concerned about when he made a distinction between a "full, or perfect, knowledge of the end," and "an imperfect knowledge of the end," a distinction discussed, in part, above. My point is this, and it is certainly one of Aquinas' as well; only when this distinction is made are we able to "distinguish between the perfect and imperfect voluntary act."

> The voluntary in a full sense follows on a perfect knowledge of the end which is had insofar as one is able, once the end has been apprehended, to deliberate concerning the end and the means of achieving it and to direct or not direct himself to the end. A lesser sense of the voluntary follows on the imperfect knowledge of the end, which is had when the agent apprehends the end but does not deliberate, being immediately moved toward it. Hence the voluntary in the full sense belongs only to rational agents, while animals may be said to act voluntarily in a lesser sense of the term.

Here is one of St. Thomas' most cogent epistemological statements. However, we must be careful in our reading to qualify a number of the implications. For instance, when he speaks of perfect knowledge he is referring, of course, to that knowledge gained because the mind has experienced its object and therefore found meaning. He is not using the word perfect in an absolute sense; this he attributes to First Cause, or God. This perfect knowledge is knowledge of the end or what is now known of the reasons in cause, the purpose of the existent, and what can be gained when meaning is found. There are degrees of the apprehension of knowledge, but not by means of the rational process; rather, by means of the intellective process, namely, the affective, cognitive and conative constructs. End is actualized when the meaning and significance of end is seen in the reasons in cause. To achieve this perception the mind must deliberate (intellectively) by means of its methodology for knowing, on how it is to proceed towards knowing.

Imperfect knowledge is what is gained by the not to be trusted process of rationalization. While there is voluntary movement, it is not the same voluntary perception generated by perfect knowledge; there is movement but no deliberation. Deliberation means the intellective process is in operation; without it, knowledge is imperfect.

There is one more comment necessary in order to understand the statement of St. Thomas: ". . . the voluntary in the full sense belongs only to rational agents, . . ." It must be remembered that he makes a distinction between the rational agent—the true learner—and the learner with only imperfect knowledge, gained by the use of the rationalization process. The true rational agent is moved by the Reason inherent in the reason(s) in cause; he realizes the inadequacy of the rationalization process and makes a distinction between it and the intellective process. The rational agent is free to act or not to act, and he knows the reasons for his decision. It is within his power to will to act, or refuse the pressure of the rationalization process for him to will action. He considers it of extreme importance that he is free and thus voluntarily he is able to will not to act. This is a rational act of the rational agent using all dimensions of the intellective process in order to reach his decision and make his choice. Moreover, it is the rational agent who determines when the act is the resultant of voluntary or involuntary action of the mind.

The Involuntary Act?

While the involuntary dimensions of the act have been discussed above, there is one additional thought which we would do well to consider. We consider it, however, only as a problem in semantics.

We begin by reminding ourselves that it is not the act which is involuntary, but the action of the mind which caused or brought the act into being.

Now, then, is it possible for an act to be involuntary when the mind knows that it possesses all the knowledge necessary to do what should be done? But, doesn't do it. So I involuntarily drive carelessly when I know that it is possible for me to drive carefully? In other words, I possess the ability to be careful, but I am not using that ability. Is my action at this point involuntarily generated? Evidently, I am not willing to do better, but why? If I will not to do better, can my action be said to be involuntary? Here is a question we cannot treat lightly in our discussions.

The Moral Act

When I stated above, Evidently, I am not willing to do better, but why? I was asking the question, Wherein lies the morality in an act? It is a question we must answer before we move on.

Morality in act tells us that the mind is free to choose; that it is self-determinant and the resultant act is in process because of a psychological stand of the mind. Morality speaks to a deep commitment to responsibility; the responsible mind is the moral mind, one free to make a choice. Without freedom to choose, the mind is unwilling to accept responsibility for the decision or act. Morality here is not a consideration because the will is not free. The moral mind will act morally, out of necessity, as Aquinas never tires in reminding us. The 'out of necessity' refers, of course, to the belief of the mind in the what and why of its beliefs. Because the mind believes as it does, it wills by means of its morality.

Now we come to an interesting epistemological junction; the word-scope is beginning to change; it is necessary to decrease our speed because we are confronted by this question, If the mind wills by means of its morality, does this imply that the mind could not have done otherwise? Our contention is that the mind has been thinking morally. Now then, is it free to think in any other way? The answer is, yes. The mind can decide to act (willfully) irresponsibly. This does not at all detract from what was said above that the mind wills by means of its morality. This is the way it wills, when it wills responsibly. However, when it wills responsibly then it could not have acted otherwise. And, with respect to both decisions, we have no alternative but to say, They were caused by a self-determined mind. All of which tells us that freedom of choice is the freedom to do other than we are morally bound to do. This is one of the problems so besetting, for so long, to Mr. Nowell Smith. Nor must we forget G. E. Moore's discussion of this problem in his *Ethics*; we get the feeling, however, that Moore is uncertain about his stand; for some reason, even though he tells us the mind could have acted otherwise if it so willed or chose, he does not speak of the mind's will to act by means of its morality even though it appears that he wants to. Here, insofar as I am concerned, is the pivot of our problem of Free-Will. When will the mind will to act responsibly? When it knows it can? Or, it wills to will because of its responsibility (acceptance of) leaves no alternative? Only the self-determined mind can make this decision.

because of its responsibility (acceptance of) leaves no alternative? Only the self-determined mind can make this decision.

When the mind acts responsibly, the result is (a) morality in the act.

The Purposive Act

Morality in an act is always purposive in nature. Since we are talking here about the psychological act, the resultant of the intellective process and not the pre-determined physical set which may make the act other than what was intended by the mind, our concern is not with the mechanistic factor in the pre-determiner.

When the mind wills (responsibly or irresponsibly), it is with purpose. What this says is that will knows what it is about. In other words, it knows what it is doing and why. And because it knows, it wills but only because it has believed in what it knows. This, too, is a process; as process, there is movement; the mind gathers momentum because of the desire to actualize what the belief portends. As the mind wills, it causes the act to become. What we really have here is the mind acting.

Before we define what we mean by acting, further explanation is necessary pertaining to the purposive act described in the paragraph above. The mind knows, and because the mind does know, the will knows. It knows that if I shake the tree (and the conditions are right) the kite will come down. The act is purpose: I will to shake the tree in order to get the kite down. Now it believes that if the tree is shaken, and the tree must be shaken to get the kite down, the kite will come down. It knows there are no obstructions on the kite or in the tree. In other words, there is no known reason why the kite will not come down if the tree is shaken. Therefore, the mind wills the arms to shake the tree.

This is acting. What do we mean by it?

Acting Freely

When the will knows there are no obstructions, as cited in the above illustration, there is knowledge because there is thought. In the intellective process, there is thought before action, as well as during the action; this is the mind acting. It permits us to define the relationship between thought and the acting process. Because the will acts, the mind has already assumed its role as a self-determiner. This means that acting now follows thought and its constructs; acting is the process of actualizing thought patterns.

This position can be clarified if we look for a moment at some thought patterns of Plato. Plato speaks to our problem in his *Republic*. Before his position is stated, however, I wish to note that while most often he speaks of spirit and many translators prefer this usage, I am convinced that the correct translation is will. The context of his usage, I believe, bears me out on this matter.

It will be remembered that Plato divides the soul into three parts. The faculty of thought and knowledge is reason. Thought acts on its decisions, namely, will and appetite. This does not imply that reason is, in a sense, independent, reason is dependent upon will; for the self-determined mind, the will not to be acting is unreasonable and not in keeping with the intent of reason. Here is another source which speaks to the ambiguous state, the paradox of free-will. Will is determined if the mind allows itself to be determined; will is a determiner if the mind assumes its role as a self-determiner. Only in its role as a self-determiner is the mind free to the extent that it wills to act, actualizing its thought patterns. It is the agent who is, or is not, free, thereby enabling the mind to act.

The Spontaneous Act

The corrective here is found in a sentence above: for the will not to be acting is unreasonable and not in keeping with the intent of reason. There is an attribute of the will which makes the acting a spontaneous force and which, in a sense, characterizes will as movement. It is will which acts upon the decision to will or not to will. Its position as an integral part of the intellective process gives it a functional role together with the other constructs of the mind, namely, the affective and cognitive.

Spontaneity, in its relation to will and acting, is best described in these terms: reason possesses intent; to actualize this intent, the actualization process becomes the intellective process; here is movement; to actualize intent is to will activity. Spontaneity is present in every act of mind.

Reason possesses intent; when the mind reasons, one of the decisions it must make is to determine whether or not the Reason within the reasoning process is sufficient for it to will what is intended. The mind is now functioning as a self-determiner; it must decide what it will do. Spontaneity of activity is dependent upon the meaningfulness of Reason and its impact upon the will. The uncertainty of the spontaneous epistemological thrust is now dependent upon the mind's development of intent in relation to the intent of reason. Spontaneity comes with the decision to act because intent has been found meaningful and a thing of value. Spontaneity becomes a characteristic of will when will forms a dependent relationship upon reason and its conditions.

3. Action and Mental Behavior: A Premise

Mental behavior is the action of the mind by means of the intellective process; the process begins with at least a degree of consciousness; it is consciousness which moves the mind to process toward intellection and determine its behavior, and not by a physical explanation of a purely mental act. Mental behavior is what it is because of the choices it makes. There is action in choice; because of the nature of choice. Mental behavior has no alternative but to come into being.

Mental Behavior and Choice

The question to which I am going to address myself is this, When I make a choice, what is the nature of my mental behavior? To know what our problem is, we cite a case study.

Certain decisions were reached before the final decision was made to write this book. Now, then, we come to a pivotal question, did I know what my decision was going to be, before I decided to write the book? Only in the sense that I knew I would write the book if certain conditions made it possible, such as, completing the research and finding adequate time in the teaching schedule for the writing. In addition, I did not know before the *if*, if my mind was ready to write, or health would permit the strain. All of this speaks, in part, to the question of mental behavior. Let us be more specific. Did I choose to write the book before I knew if the conditions would permit the writing, or, because the conditions would make it possible? Why must it be an either-or problem? Did I know what I would decide if the conditions were right? Maybe this was one of the decisions made before the final decision. Could I have chosen to write the book if the conditions permitted, so that I did know what I would decide to do? Certainly. Could I have chosen to write the book after I had determined if the conditions were permissable? Only if the conditions had been favorable. If the conditions had been unfavorable, the conditions (such as no time available because of a heavy teaching schedule) themselves would have removed the freedom to choose.

What does this say about mental behavior? Perhaps a more concise way of asking the question would be, Is this a matter of mental behavior or, is it more correct to say, choice behavior? It is conceivable that my choice, dependent upon my decision, was to write the book regardless of the conditions. Then I certainly would know what my decision would be but, which, likewise, would mean the need to change at least one of the conditions such as, reducing my teaching load. But, even this confronts us with a contingency: *if* it is possible to write. What the mind is doing here is being expressed in the kind of behavior which modifies, in one way or another, potentiality.

Moreover, if I decide to write regardless of whether or not my teaching load is reduced, will modify or completely change other conditions, such as, getting along with less sleep. We can see the movement of the will here; the decision has been made to write because of the value-meaning it brings; it is given a priority over conditions which have been posited, recognized for their value, but now determined of less-value than the writing of the book.

Mental behavior speaks to the right of the self-determined mind to make these value judgments. Every decision is based on a value judgement, and every value judgment is based on a value condition. There is a closely knit logic in this. The mind is intimately involved in validating its own behavior; it is aware of the heavy responsibilities resident in all matters related to choice; the mind holds itself responsible for its behavior (its acts); this is what we mean by mental behavior.

Does this speak to questions of certainty? That is, am I certain, then, what my decision will be? The above paragraphs do address themselves to this question.

What about the problem of behavioral decisions which are causally determined? The point on which the mind would then concentrate, would be to determine if it is acting passively or actively. In either case, the decision is determined; either by forces external to the mind, or, the mind acting as cause. Here is another instance in which the role of choice behavior is seen in even clearer lines.

One final question. Is it possible for the mind to be unaware of its choice behavior? Not if the mind is functioning as a self-determiner. There is always the possibility that the mind is not aware of the changes made for it, and the consequent behavior, when it is passive and not involved in its own decision making. I say its own decision making because even in its passive role, it has decided not to decide for itself.

Excusable Behavior

In re-reading the foregoing pages, there is a question which continues to linger near the fringes of our discussion on mental behavior. The question may be worded like this, Is there mental behavior which may be categorized as excusable? We find the need to answer this question before moving on.

First of all, let me refer to a basic premise in the foregoing discussion, namely, that true mental behavior is always responsible for its acts; in order to be held responsible, it must be free to make its choices. To excuse behavior, then, it is logical to suggest that the mind under these conditions cannot be held accountable, for it is subject to determinants beyond its control. This means that these determinants, whatever they might be, allow for no choices to be made by the mind. What the mind is forced to do because it has no choice in the matter is behavior which may be labelled as excusable.

There is another thought here which must be examined, as well. Whenever the mind acting as will is unable to function in this capacity, its mental behavior may be said to be excusable. This is clear and leaves no room for question. But, what about the mind (here thought of as totality) which acts against its will? Is the mental behavior then excusable? This last question is a bit redundant. At least until we have answered the first question. Let us rephrase it. Is it possible for the will to act against the will? Not if the mind is still free to function as mind, that is, with the affective, cognitive and conative constructs fully operational. If the mind is not free, then the will does not act against itself, because it is unable to function in the first place.

All of this brings to the front another dimension of the problem. We posit this setting. Is it possible for the mind to be determined by conditions which do not make it possible to function freely, therefore as will, yet remain knowledgable to the extent that it knows that what it is doing is against its will, that is, if it were free to act otherwise, it would do so? The answer is, yes, of course. However, this does not mean that in this setting the mind is acting against its will. The will, free to act, never acts against itself. It must be remembered that the will acts when it is free, and it acts responsibly, according to whatever values it has validated as good. When the mind knows that what is happening is against its will, but it has no power to control, the act must be recognized as: the mind knowing, but not acting; it does not act against its will, but, rather, it knows that it is against its will. This distinction must be kept in mind in our total discussion of mental behavior.

Intentionality is a key concept here. This has been seen in the role of the mind functioning as will. The mind intends, but if it is not free to operate according to its intentionality and by means of the will, it is not responsible for the actions which it is conditioned to fulfill. There is a perspective in intentionality, one which has been carefully cognized; because of this, we can say that the mind acts from the vantage of its intentionality. The mind free to do this, is the self-determinant mind, free to act, and one which knows that it is responsible for its actions. Furthermore, it is upon the intentions of the mind that the will acts; this is true because in the process of cognizing intentionality, one thing required by the will is the validation of intent. That is, the mind decides that what is willed, will be good for the moral agent, because of what the mind has found to be good for itself. What determines the criteria for this goodness is covered elsewhere in this book.

Is there excusable behavior, then? Yes, if the mind is being determined; the self-determined mind does not accept excuse for its own behavior.

Human Behavior and Its Relation to Cause and Effect

To speak of human behavior is, in most instances, to refer to physical movement; that is, what the moral agent does, physically. While this is the most common contextual frame of reference, the foregoing discussion has alerted us to facets of human behavior which bring many questions into being. For instance, when we speak of human behavior, are we justified in any sense, to limit its definition to physical movement or reaction? Not at all. For then we must ask, Is physical behavior triggered by physical cause or confrontation? Here the answer again is, No. Certainly physical behavior is caused, but under conditions in which mind is free to function, the physical organism is dependent upon the mind to furnish the signals directing its behavior. When conditions do not permit such freedom of movement and activity for the mind, the mind is there determined and cannot be held responsible for the actions of the body. Such restrictions cancel the intentionality of will.

An illustration is in order here. My foot is resting on the heat radiator in my study. A few moments ago I crossed my legs and placed the right foot on the radiator. This is a comfortable position for me as I write. All my action up to this point has been intended. What has been done has been willed, because of the conditions which permit comfort, and because of the value I have placed upon this writing position. The totality of such movement is my human behavior. There has been physical activity, but it has been mind-directed, caused by a decision and willed to fulfillment or implementation. But a moment ago, I very quickly lifted my foot from the radiator; because of the heat, my foot was close to being burned. In a sense, I anticipated that such action may be necessary. The conditions are these: it is winter, quite cold, the room is very warm which means that for the room to be as warm as it is, the radiator must be throwing a great deal of heat. To put my foot on a very warm radiator, in time, means there will be some physical reactions. Now, all of this is mental movement and evaluation; my mental behavior, if it were summer, would be quite different. In this case, cause and the reasons which make cause cause, are readily apparent. All of this, of course, gives evidence of an active mind, one which is free to move and react because of its ability to cognize and will.

At times, though, the mind is surprised by fact, and this happens when it has allowed itself to slip into that epistemological twilight zone between activity and passivity. That is, when the mind is not doing its job, and is not alert to its responsibilities. In a sense, we are even justified in saying that when the mind is surprised by fact, it has allowed itself to become, in part, determined. At such times, the physical behavior will be a reaction the cause of which has not been processed and handled by the mind, and therefore, not willed.

The self-determined mind is vitally concerned that it serve as the intermediary between an external cause and physical movement of the mind's body. This means that it finds it necessary to interiorize the reasons in cause so that the signals given to the body will provide the right action and assure that good will result. As a matter of fact, so concerned is the mind that in this process, the mind itself assumes the role of secondary cause and feels secure only when human behavior is what it does when its directives are taken from the mind alone.

In the final analysis, it would be totally wrong to say that the self-determined mind remains the intermediary between an external cause and physical movement of the mind's body. This role is discarded when it assumes the role of secondary cause. At this point in the relationship, mediation is no longer required. As secondary cause, the process of intellection now begins to function.

This position, I am sure, is quite distressing to the strict determinist. So that he will not be in question about my assumptions, let me, in summary fashion, state the presuppositions as I see them.

1. Human behavior, when the mind is free to function as a self-determiner, is mental behavior; there are physical actions, all of which are purposive in nature.

2. Every action has a cause; if it is natural causality, and beyond the power of control by mind, such causality determines a behavior, the responsibility for which is not assumed by the mind. Purpose may realize itself in human behavior only when the reason(s) in just cause (natural) is actualized by the self-determined mind. That is, the effect of cause is realized as purposive in nature, the mind now acting in the role of the determiner, deciding and willing what the confrontation will mean (allowed to mean) for itself. Effect for the self-determined mind remains in the realm of the probable until it is willed into actualization.

Even in natural causality there is reason, therefore purpose. But this does not mean that its purpose will be actualized in human behavior. If the mind allows itself to be determined by natural causality without serving as an intermediary, human behavior may then be other than what the mind would will.

3. As every action has a cause, every action is purposive, both in First and secondary causes. In each case, however, the mind has a different responsibility for the realization of this purpose.

The Problem of Motivation for the Self-Determined Mind

What motivates the mind to function differently, first in relation to First cause, and then to itself as it becomes second cause? Why is there a different responsibility?

From what has been said above, the assumption that all behavior is motivational, perhaps could stand on its own feet. But, the statement, as it stands alone, leaves something to be desired. First of all, it needs clarification. Do we mean that all behavior serves as motivator? That is, because of what the behavior is, because of its nature, it is able to motivate something else? This would make behavior a cause, probably secondary cause. Or, do we mean that all behavior is motivational because it is not cause, but has been caused; something like mind or a natural causality has made behavior (the act) what it is? The self-determined mind would identify with the second of these interpretations, naturally; but we must not be too quick to discard one insight which may be gained from the first interpretation. For the self-determined mind, human behavior is mental behavior; it is caused; but, when it loses its identity as an object, that is, when behavior as object and mind as subject fuse (human behavior becomes mental behavior), behavior, as mental activity, becomes cause. This is an important premise for the self-determined mind. It requires this kind of freedom in order to actualize its own potentiality, part of which is the control of its own behavior.

Even in all this discussion we have not, as yet, answered the question, What motivates the mind to function differently, first in relation to First Cause, and then to itself as it becomes second cause? The answer is implied in the preceding paragraph but perhaps it requires one more degree of explanation. The self-determined mind recognizes, in the first place, that unless it makes the choice to be a determiner, it will be determined by a natural causality which is governed by purpose and meaning, but which remains impersonal in its modes of identification until the human mind personalizes the relationship. This is the unique responsibility of the human mind. Only the human mind can accomplish it. When the human mind has identified and actualized the reason(s) in First Cause (learning their meaning), the process of experiencing (personalizing) purpose is complete. The responsibility of the human mind in this relationship is complete.

All of this is not required, as a responsibility, of the mind in its relationship to itself. The personalization process has already been completed. Moreover, the human mind cannot assume the role of second cause, until this process has been completed. Now it steps in and becomes, in its own right, natural cause; it has appropriated for its own use the reasons which make cause cause.

CHAPTER TWO

MORAL AUTHORITY

What we face here are two concepts, both of which require definition. We shall attempt to build a definition of each by raising a number of questions.

First, there is authority.

Wherein lies the source of authority? Does this source grant power to authority? Who determines place for authority? What is the relationship between responsibility and authority? Does authority reside in responsibility? Is responsibility identical with authority? Does authority, then, define its responsibility in keeping with its definition of the self, i.e., its authority? Does responsibility eliminate the idea of freedom for the self-determined mind, the mind which has the authority to act, and does act, morally? Does this imply that the self-determined mind is the source of its own authority? Is it its own authority? Does the concept of moral authority allow for this assumption of the self-determined mind?

We have now prepared our mind to ask the same kinds of questions with respect to the idea of morality in its relation to authority.

Wherein lies the source of authority for the moral judgment? (What is moral cannot be spoken of without its referent, the judgment). Does this source of authority provide the moral judgment with the power that morality must possess in order to function as a judgment? What affect does the moral judgment have upon the relationship between responsibility and authority? Does the affect provide the relationship with a new perspective? Or, a new responsibility? What is the source of morality for the determination of what responsibility must accept as its responsibility? What is the authority for such a determination? What is the chief characteristic of the moral judgment if responsibility is identical with authority? Whose responsibility is it to assist in the formulation of the definition of authority? Is the idea of freedom the resultant of the assumptions of the moral judgment, one of which is the authority of the self-determined mind, based on a source other than the self?

Moral authority, what is it? This question will be answered when each of the questions raised above has been satisfactorily studied. We take them in order of their first appearance.

Wherein lies the source of authority? To this, we add another question, What authority? And, of course, the answer is, The authority of the mind. Mind is the decision maker; in the totality of its many constructs, it wills; it is under obligation and restraint to do so; it wills, or, it wills not to do something. Here is choice inherent in every decision. *A priori* to the decision is authority to make the decision. This responsibility rests wholly with the mind. It possesses this authority because of the empirical constructs which comprise its nature, but even more so because of the responsibility it has to the learning self.

The learning self. What is it? It can be understood only when seen in relation to the answer to the next question. Wherein lies the source of authority? The mind possesses authority because First Cause is the source from which all things created (caused) receive the essence of their being.

What has been created, as finite, has been caused. What it is, is what it was intended to be by First Cause, the absolute. In the realm of the purely physical, there is a design by law, a determinism in source, for the cyclical movement of its purpose. In the realm of the psychological, there is a design by intent which provides the opportunity for the mind to choose, either to be determined, or to determine. Because of the nature of the intent of cause, as source, it is the given authority to the mind which weighs the opportunity, emphasizing the true potentiality of what the self-determined mind can become.

Because of what the source is, and the kind of assistance given by Cause to the mind, as the Essence of the Being of what is absolute, source is morality, and it is this morality which is given as authority to the mind in each of its epistemological relationships.

Moral authority resides in what is possible for the mind to learn, and how knowledge is attained. It is the learning self which, because of its responsibility, as moral being, knows it must experience the object (to be learned) in order to find meaning and reach the level of understanding which will permit the mind to become self-correcting in all of its processes.

Who determines place for authority? The answer to this question is not as difficult as it may first appear. Place is the positional responsibility given by Cause to the mind as it is given the responsibility to serve as the means whereby the self learns, as well as serves as the means whereby the self functions as mind, as its relationship to every other existent external to it. Let me explain this statement. In order for the mind to learn, the relationship between itself as a being caused, must be established and then actualized (as it becomes a process). This is a dependent relationship; mind cannot function as something which has been created until it establishes a working dependency upon reason(s) in cause. From this relationship alone the mind receives its purpose for existence, as well as the means from which it draws its essence to become an intellective process.

When this relationship has been actualized, the mind knows its place in the schemata between First Cause and everything which serves as potentiality for the mind to come to know. When the mind knows its place, it has realized the authority it possesses; it is an authority which speaks to the proposition: it is only the human mind which can come to know; First Cause has chosen it to become a second cause, the only means whereby what has been created can understand itself, as well as understand all other external existents.

Written into the essence of the relationship between First and second cause is the morality which is the absolute. It is a morality which can be accepted by the mind and thus become a self-determined mind or, rejected, forcing the self of the mind to become something determined by that which is external to it. The whole question of moral authority is pivotal for the mind as it wills, by means of its choices, its own destiny. This is one part of its responsibility as a self-directing second cause. It has no other source than First Cause, other than the self, to which it can turn, to meet its dependency needs.

What is the relationship between responsibility and authority? We have posited the authority of the mind; we shall be returning to this position from time to time, especially in its relationship to responsibility. First, however, we wish to speak of the authority which is First Cause. It is the authority which is identical with First Principles and the Absolute.

To speak of authority and First Cause is to speak of First Cause as authority, but only in its relation to responsibility. This is a relationship quite different from the authority of the human mind and responsibility. In this case, the mind, even with authority, is free to ignore its responsibility as a moral agent. This is not true for the Mind of First Cause. For one thing, its nature is different from the nature of the human mind. For another, its responsibility is different. With respect to First Cause, both authority and responsibility is that which makes First Cause First Creator. As absolute, authority and responsibility is absolute. As absolute and Creator, it is Mind with absolute knowledge; thus it knows what it must do, why, and how the goal is to be realized. It has no freedom other than what it gives itself by means of its authority and responsibility.

For the human mind, as second cause and creator, it has no freedom other than what it accepts from First Cause as its authority and responsibility. This process of acceptance or rejection is epistemological in nature, and one of the initiatory steps in human learning. Without this step, the human mind remains but a determined entity, a pawn to the existents external to its nature.

Does authority reside in responsibility? For the First Cause, the answer is, Yes. To this we must add, responsibility also resides in authority. For the human mind, the story can be different, if the mind so wills it. The authority to know is the perogative given to the human mind by the Source of knowledge. Within this prerogative lies the means by which the mind is able to actualize the authority; that is, to know. Again, that is, if it accepts its responsibility of learning so that it can come to know. This means, accepting the responsibility inherent in learning methodologies, as well as bringing the self to the point of willing the mind (even though it is the mind itself which does this) to learn. To will to learn is to determine the value and application of the learning objects' meaningfulness. Without this, the mind probably will choose to will not to learn. It, then, has decided not to accept its responsibility. The mind is also aware that one of its greatest responsibilities is to know the true nature of its responsibilities. These can be known only in relation to what First Cause makes possible by way of learning potentialities in existence itself, and the willingness of the human mind to exercise its epistemological ingenuity for learning. Is responsibility identical with authority? In a sense, this question has been answered, with one exception. The concept authority possesses the characteristic of growing as the human mind increases its acceptance of the need to accept even greater responsibility. Because of this characteristic, the mind gives its authority because it accepts responsibility. Because responsibility has been accepted, the mind possesses the opportunity to exert greater authority. It remains an option; whether or not it is used, is a matter of will.

Does authority, then, define its responsibility in keeping with its definition of the self, i.e., its authority? The implications of this question are such to force us to shift our epistemological gears. The real impact of the question is this: to define the nature of the self of the mind is to determine whether or not it wills to be determined or (to be) self-determined. If the decision is to be determined, the mind thereby accepting its role as something passive, its responsibility as a moral agent is practically non-existent. However, if the choice is to be a self-determiner, the mind becomes aware of its responsibility to the self in order to become a self-determiner. The point is this. The mind is free to make the decision if it wishes to be free or determined. This, in itself, tells itself all it needs to know about its responsibility to its authority, and the opportunities which may be present if the authority (the option) is to be exercised. Does it will to become passive or active? If active, its authority will grow with the acceptance of greater responsibility and responsibility will grow with the acceptance of greater authority.

Our next question is a natural one. Does responsibility eliminate the idea of freedom for the self-determined mind, the mind which has the authority to act, and does act, morally? This time the answer is, No. We return to a basic assumption, that is, it is only the self-determined mind which is free to choose its epistemological destiny. Since it is either determined, or becomes a self-determiner, and what is determined cannot be free, the mind, if it wills to be free, must first will to be self-determined. Freedom is the opportunity to make use of the potentialities of the mind; when it makes use of these opportunities, it is exercising its option of responsibility and acts morally.

The idea of freedom is the opportunity presented by First Cause to the human mind as the possibility for self-actualization. In other words, Cause is saying by means of the essence of its relationship (the object for knowing): Here is your potentiality, realizable because of the freedom you possess, to know. Potentiality speaks of option; the human mind is free to disregard it if it wishes; however, if it does, it wills not to know. The act, then, is not a moral one. The moral act means the mind is exercising its moral responsibility (option) to know.

Does this imply that the self-determined mind is the source of its own authority? We have stated that the mind is the decision-maker. We have also said that the mind has been created and exists in its potentiality, but, it possesses the authority and responsibility to create itself and, in the process, to become second cause. Now, we must ask, If the mind exists in its potentiality and when that potentiality is actualized, mind is in the process of becoming, we then must conclude, as we do elsewhere in this book, that mind is, at all times, dependent upon that which provides it with its essence. Mind functions only in relation to a referent; it must have something upon which to operate. Whatever serves as this essence, is the authority which grants the opportunity for the mind to function. This is Cause.

From this point, we move on and say, when the mind has willed to be self-determined, the bases upon which it places its moral responsibilities, now begin to serve as the secondary authority which operates by means of the epistemological methods for knowing (learning) chosen by the mind.

Prime authority resides in First Cause; secondary authority resides in the mind which has chosen to be a self-determiner.

Is it its own authority? In one sense, no. Mind, to be mind, remains in a state of dependency upon external objects (those created by First Cause). This dependency does not change even though the external object, by means of language and its symbols, is interiorized by the mind. When the mind begins to create itself, and a new created order comes into being, in this process, the mind is building for itself an epistemological authority upon which its methodology is empirically determined.

Does the concept of moral authority allow for this assumption of the self-determined mind? Not only does the moral authority allow for this assumption, but it is dependent upon it as the source of its own meaning. It must not be forgotten that the mind is what it learns so that it can become more than it was. The mind becomes self-determined only because it wills activity rather than passivity. It wills self-determination when it learns the potentiality of this stance, and makes the choice to become what is good.

We have now completed the first set of questions, those related specifically to authority. The emphasis now is to be placed on the idea of the moral. Many of the following questions follow closely on the heels of questions answered above. The reader will do well to draw parallels in order to complete the epistemological tapestry.

Wherein lies the source of authority for the moral judgment? (What is moral cannot be spoken of without its referent, the judgment). The idea of the moral has often been made a plaything by epistemologists. Many have clothed it in metaphysical trappings, and thereby have disguised it, not allowing it the freedom of intellective movement it deserves. Those who have toyed with it, have also suggested that its motive is a bit elusive, making it almost impossible to define. We shall not toy with it, believe that it is elusive, or dress it in clothing other than its own. For the idea of the moral is the teleological perspective instilled within its very nature by Cause itself. The logic behind this move by Cause is clear and concise in its purpose. Since the mind is free to choose its epistemological destiny, the reason for whatever choice is made must also be balanced; that is, the mind can choose to be determined, that is, assume a passive role in the learning process. Upon what is this choice based? Certainly not upon the sense of the moral authority confronting the human mind instilled by Cause. On the contrary; the mind now wills what it conceives of as good, carrying another meaning and based upon another source, such as the desire only for not being held responsible for its own destiny. You see, it is possible to will the unwillingness to be responsible. The mind has the freedom to make such a decision, but the decision is not based on the moral authority of First Cause. First Cause wants the human mind to be responsible, and does everything possible to encourage it to accept this perspective. Thus, it provides the balance, the understanding of what is really good, based not upon the subjectivity of the human mind in the exclusion of reason in Cause, but, on the objectivity resident in Reason in Cause. Herein lies the foundation of the idea of the moral; whatever decision is made by the mind, it is a judgment based on a definitive relationship to the moral authority which mirrors the intentionality of First Cause. Also, whatever decision is made reflects the nature of that relationship as one rejecting the moral authority, or accepting the moral directives designed for the purpose of assisting the mind to become self-determining. The idea of the moral is not originated in the human mind; this is present first only in First Cause; when the mind has become self-determined, its judgments will then reflect what it now has made its own, the epistemological morality, tried and tested, which continues to generate self-correcting judgments which lead to continued learning.

Does this source of authority provide the moral judgment with the power that morality must possess in order to function as a judgment? Here is a different kind of question. To answer it first demands that we define the concept of power. The first thing to remember is that it is the moral judgment that provides morality with power. What we are asking is this, What is the power possessed by morality? Morality is the value placed upon each existent in its creation by First Cause, and which is reflected in each existent as a potential to be known by the human mind as it makes the value its own. Morality is the opportunity to experience the purpose of creation by creation and actualizing its meaning. The power of morality is lodged in the meaningfulness of the learning momentum, by means of which the mind appropriates unto itself the intentionality of First Cause. Since the mind, at all times, is making judgments, which, hopefully, are self-correcting in nature, it is the will of Cause that its teleological perspective becomes willed by the human mind by means of the intellective process. The incentive for the mind to will is received from the power inherent in movement which is the act of decision and therefore choice. To will from the source of morality which is First Cause, is to will from the value of source, namely, the reason(s) in Cause; to will from a morality which is a determined mind, is to will from the value generated by a self in relation only to itself.

What affect does the moral judgment have upon the relationship between responsibility and authority? It is responsibility which is most highly influenced by the moral judgment. It is the moral judgment and its implications which will determine whether or not the mind accepts its responsibility to make use of the epistemological opportunities for learning proffered by Cause. Because a moral judgment has been made, the choice among values has also been made, one of which speaks to a decision as to whether or not the implications suggestive of responsibility are worth pursuing. The mind is not morally-bound to accept the value opportunities placed in each existent by Cause. If these opportunities are not accepted, the mind then moves forward according to self-generated values, arising from within its own value system. In this sense, judgments are always moral because they possess a referent and are based upon a willed decision. Thus, it is the authority of First Cause which serves as the momentum for the mind in its learning processes, or the authority of a mind moved only by those things external to it and which demand passivity. First Cause, as authority and the source of morality, moves the mind and its essence to an activity leading to self-determination and the realization of meaning expressed in the intentionality of cause.

What is determined has its thinking done for it; the mind which does its own thinking by using its intellective process creates an authority which now justifies its movement and is constantly correcting its perspective by the judgments it makes.

Or, a new responsibility? Indeed. Whenever a perspective is corrected, the responsibility to validate that new perspective is always there. Moreover, with responsibility comes greater responsibility; this is an integral part of the learning process. As we learn by experiencing experience, we make learning self-correcting by assuming even greater responsibility toward what can become greater opportunities.

What is the source of morality for the determination of what responsibility must accept as its responsibility? We found it necessary to ask this question because of our discussion in the paragraph above. The self-determined mind knows that it must learn in order to learn more. There is a very active perspective here; it is a recognition that in every existent lies a tremendous potential in what can be known. To accept the responsibility to know as much as possible is to move toward the actualization of First Intention. What has been created, has been created for a reason. The responsible mind is the self-determined mind, determined, by way of its intellective processes, to learn what can be learned about an existent. As the mind accepts this kind of responsibility, it becomes aware of what it can come to mean if greater responsibility is accepted. This is the only means by which the mind grows by learning.

What is the authority for such a determination? Here, again, the authority is no different from what has been cited above. The same principles are in effect; the self-determined mind determines what it will will, as it accepts its responsibility to know by experiencing intentionality. Intentionality is its own value construct, the same which it is endeavoring to make known by enabling the mind to experience its potentiality for meaning.

What is the chief characteristic of the moral judgment if responsibility is identical with authority? We have answered the second half of the question beginning with the conjunctive *if*, above. To answer the question in the first half is to preface the answer with these thoughts inherent in a position is the judgment. As long as I believe that there is a reason (purpose) for whatever I do, because I do what I do, the what is the actualization of judgment. Judgment makes it possible for the mind to actualize itself in act; the morality of the judgment expresses the stance that it has been necessary for the mind to go to some source for its authority, either to Cause as Creator, or, to the self, as created. The chief characteristic of the moral judgment then, is that every judgment is based on some moral premise, the source of which is determined by the mind itself.

Whose responsibility is it to assist in the formulation of the definition of authority? Here, in capsule form, is the reason-to-be for epistemology. It is the pivotal concept in the learning-knowing relationship. In the final analysis, to know means I have learned the authority (meaning) of the essence of the object, in the subject-object relationship. That is, I have learned the intended meaning of an existent, as that meaning is completely identical with the existent as determined by Cause alone. Resident in meaning is the authority which makes it what it is because it is so intended. Essentially, when we speak of this kind of relationship, it is no different from our contention that existence cannot be conceived of separately from essence, and because there is essence, there is existence. Because an existent *is*, it has been created, and as something created, it *was* created for a purpose, and with purpose in Mind. The authority resident in what exists, exists, because that authority was given it by Cause. The responsibility for first authority rests with First Cause. The responsibility to define authority and what it means and implies, lies with the human mind as it is confronted with the need to determine the nature of the relationship between itself and

First Cause. When that relationship has been defined, the source of the morality and its epistemological ethic will have been located.

Is the idea of freedom the resultant of the assumptions of the moral judgment, one of which is the authority of the self-determined mind, based on a source other than the self? Most definitely. First Cause has as its objective assisting the human mind to learn by responding, in a very active way, to those things which cause makes possible to be learned. To succeed, the mind needs freedom; the freedom to contemplate by thinking, experiment, devise learning methodologies, analyze and weigh evidence, to use whatever exists to assist in the process, to create from what has been created, and to make at least semi-final judgments. Implied in such freedom lies the assumption that in every object resides learning potentiality; that is, a potentiality to determine what the object is, but also, what it can become when the created mind now becomes a creator, bringing into being new relationships, and, therefore, new being. It is the morality of a knowing which comes from learning the meaning of cause.

CHAPTER THREE

FREEDOM

The Concept of Freedom

It is a common failure among epistemologists to draw this conclusion: "either human actions are the outcomes of causes, like any other events, or they are random fortuitous incidents." As if this is not side-stepping the real issues, they insist upon adding: "in neither case can they be proper subjects for moral judgments." Let us look at each of these propositions.

First, "either human actions are the outcomes of causes, like any other events . . ." In this instance, all we must do is (to) remove the word *either.* Human actions *are* the outcomes of causes. This is not to say that the actions are always voluntary or the agent is necessarily in control of the cause. However, we do contend there is a cause for every human action, whether or not the mind realizes it or, is able to actualize it by pin-pointing the reason in cause. There is always a reason for *whatever* happens. This premise is based on the assumption that every existent (with the exception of the absolute) is dependent upon another existent for purpose, meaning and existence. The only existing entity is the absolute. Whenever there is a total dependency relationship, and the nature of that relationship changes, inherent in the principles which unite the two entities is reason in cause. With change there is cause because something has altered the nature of the willing principle. When cause assumes an impersonal stance, the human mind now concerns itself with what it can cognize, namely, the implications of cause. The human will is not adequate to handle the impersonal nature of a force in nature, but it can handle the resultant of the cause as it affects the human mind and the totality of the self.

Second, "or they are random fortuitous incidents." Here, again, human actions may be done without pre-meditation; this is not to imply that even fortuitous incidents do not have causes attached to them. There is reason behind every action; whether or not it is a logical reason, or intended is beside the point. Things do not happen by themselves. The leaf does not just drop from the stem; it is pulled, or its life's sap has been withdrawn and it is now dry, the wind may dislodge it, any one of which, or a combination of all, may be the cause of action in the inanimate world. The same is true for the human being. Moments ago one of my legs reflexed, without intention or purpose on my part. Nevertheless, there was a reason, or a number of reasons why the leg moved. The reason is inherent in cause.

Third, "in neither case can they be proper subjects for moral judgments." We must be careful to qualify our response. If the mind is not responsible for evaluating the implications of an act brought about by even such a thing as an impersonal cause, then the proposition would be true. The human mind is constantly being confronted by the need to act (or, even forced to act) because of situations not created by the self. Epistemologically speaking, this is beside the point. Regardless of what happens to the self (the implications for change) the mind is responsible for its reactions if the mind is allowed to function by means of its intellective process. This requires of the mind the need then, to form a judgment which carries moral overtones. Whenever the mind is confronted with the need to make a decision and choose from among alternatives, it must possess absolute freedom to make such choices. If this freedom does not exist, the mind is unable to function by means of the epistemological balance among the affective, cognitive and conative domains of the intellective process.

What affirms freedom? The simple fact that I can do what I will? This is, "without restraint or compulsion?" Hardly. Simply because of the ever-contending problem of reason in cause. This factor is forever complicating the clarity of what we conceive of as the freedom of the will. While we have shown the power the mind does possess in relation to cause, regardless of its impersonal or personal nature, freedom exists only in the relation between the mind and the implications of cause.

The Mind in its Consciousness of Freedom

Of course the mind is aware of the freedom it possesses. Awareness is an indication of a degree of consciousness. Moreover, the mind is conscious of itself as possessing the means whereby it is able to will. Our premise is that the mind, because it knows it possesses freedom in relation to what cause implies, that is, the responsibility to make a choice, is conscious of the fact it *will* do something even if it is a decision to do nothing. Our premise is not affected even though "we have good evidence that the action in question is brought about by causes quite other than the subject's free choice."

This is not a feeling of freedom of which we speak. All facets of the intellective process are at work here, not simply the affective domain. If freedom has any meaning it comes only by means of the mind experiencing its potentiality; the mind knows it possesses the freedom to choose from among alternatives presented as implications stemming from cause.

Freedom and the Problem of the Contra-Causal

Perhaps the two preceding paragraphs are not clear in what they are attempting to say. If not, the following discussion should help us think our way through the problem.

If the action is brought about by causes other than the subject's free choice, our first conclusion might be that the subject is not responsible for the action. This is true. We have discussed the ramifications of this in many places in this book. Due to natural causes, namely, high winds, in spite of the stabilizers, caused the good ship the QEII to roll, throwing me against a wall and bruising a shoulder. I was not responsible for the action of the ship, but was I responsible for the implications of the action, which might have caused me to act other than what I had done? After all, I was conscious of the storm and the rolling of the ship, as well as the potentiality of danger from walking because of the conditions. I could have decided to remain in my cabin safely snuggled in my bunk. There was no need to leave the cabin. Are we not able to say that I assumed the responsibility of the implications of a walk on deck. What if there was the question of necessity? Supposing it was necessary to reach the physician immediately? Would our basic problem be changed? Not at all. What if I decided to chance the walk knowing that the chance of injury was great? Here, again, the place of implication and responsibility changes not one iota.

Could I have done otherwise? With respect to what was happening to the ship? No, such a thought is nonsense. Could I have done otherwise with respect to what the ship was doing to me? Yes, of course. What I do will depend, in part, on how I conceive of my responsibility in relation to the implications of what is being caused.

The Criteria of Freedom

If the above is true, there must be some criteria of knowledge. What are they?

We have stated the first above, namely, the mind knows rather than feels it is free in relation to the implications of cause. Also, it knows it is not free (responsibility-wise) for actions beyond its control or contrary to its choice. The very idea of freedom is not even considered relevant when applied to an action over which the mind has no control and is therefore not responsible.

The second of our criteria evolves from the first. The mind knows when it is free and, in a position to exercise its responsibility; moreover, it knows that it is not a matter of freedom when it comes to an action towards which it has no responsibility other than when it must assure responsibility for implications.

While we do not question the fact there are degrees of knowledge, truth, comprehension and consciousness, we do deny there are degrees of freedom. There are no gray areas here, all black and white. The mind is free to make a choice, or it is not.

Freedom and the Excuse of Determinism

To suggest that we are free "only if determinism is false" is to have missed the point completely with respect to our foregoing discussion. In the first place, it is incorrect to even suggest that determinism is false. The world and its essence is governed by a determinism, the nature of which is dependent upon either the reason(s) in First and second Cause, or the will stance of the human mind. Moore is correct when he says that the freedom of the human mind is compatible with determinism. We insist that freedom is existent only in relation to the implication, that is, when the mind wills its own freedom. Even then, we have a determinism, for the mind becomes a self-determiner. We have no reason to suggest there is a false determinism or, even to allow the thought that determinism (in all its stark boldness) can be the excuse why the mind is not free to make choices. The mind, in its capacity as a self-determiner, is exercising its responsibility based upon a specific ethical and moral point of view.

There has been a reason for our use of the word excuse in its relation to determinism. Moreover, there is a logic behind the use of the word responsibility in the sentence above. While we do not intend to become swallowed up in the argument, which often cites Hume as the source of the problem concerning the liberty of spontaneity, we are, nevertheless, forced to take into consideration the overtones. For instance, what about the need "to punish people for actions they were caused to perform, actions whose occurrence were in principle predictable on the basis of remote causes?" To continue: "Surely such punishment would be morally barbaric! On moral grounds therefore, we ought to repeat this fake sense of freedom; it is incompatible with civilized moral standards."

If the above statements were true, punishment as such, meted out, would be barbaric. But, again, all of this is entirely beside the point. A case in point.

I am walking on the promenade deck of the QEII. The winds are strong and the ship is in a mild roll. A man is coming from the opposite direction and, as we meet, the roll of the ship literally throws me into the other man and he is knocked off his feet. Here was an action which I was caused to perform, an action whose occurrence was in principle predictable on the basis of a remote and yet meaningful cause. You might respond by saying, because of the conditions, which were predictable, I should have taken the caution of holding on to the rail until the man passed. The point is well taken. Nevertheless, it did happen; the question of responsibility is an important one; perhaps punishment should be meted out because I was not acting in a responsible way. The argument is further strengthened because the occurrence was in principle predictable. If it was not predictable, our problem is a different one.

But, predictable or not, the mind, as a self-determiner, is always a responsible agent. If the collision occurred when the conditions were not predictable, the self-determined mind is responsible for the implications of what was caused even by an impersonal force. Is this to say that an accident, which is entirely unintentional, places the responsibility upon the agent who is the cause of the accident? Not at all. I was not the cause of the accident if the conditions were not predictable; say the wind rolled the ship before I realized what had happened; in the process of the happening, I was thrown against the man. I am still a responsible person, but not responsible for what had actually happened. I did not will myself into the other man. If I had, my responsibility would be quite evident.

We must be careful of our use of the word excuse. It can place us in a difficult epistemological position.

The Element of Faith in the Determinism Which is Freedom

What we attempted to postulate in the above paragraphs is the belief that it is not necessary, if we believe in the freedom of the will, to likewise "deny the universal reign of causality in nature." However, we do imply that, since the mind wills its own freedom, it must be conscious of the implication of what is confronting it as something which has been caused.

Is there an element of faith in all this? Faith in what? The ability of the mind to will its freedom? Faith in what freedom makes possible for the mind to achieve? Or, is it faith in First Cause or First Principle, the essence of which is reason and the designs of which are logical, governed by a purpose which reflects an absolute of mind projecting a relativity of value? Is it faith in a purity of reason, uncontaminated by the relativity of human reason, the object of this pure reason nestled securely in an empirically based data?

To speak of First Cause is to be confronted by causality in nature. It is First Cause which says, By means of what is caused, what is objective reality can be proven if there is sufficient knowledge and the will to experience the potentiality of reality.

Is there a more important question for the epistemologist then, What is cause? The well-meaning epistemologist is concerned with cause for many reasons, the first of which is his need to define it in such a way that it will differentiate cause from cause, for example, What compels us to act? and, What happens and why in the object of the mind's confrontation, in such a way that the object, if it is to be known, can be known only by means of analyzing its cause? There is cause which compels the mind to function as it does; there is cause for those things external to the mind, which affect the mind when a relationship is established between subject and object.

The human will receives its impetus from the cognitive process which is interested in its own cause for movement, but also, in the will resident in the teleological essence of purpose found in every existent. It is true, this is anthropomophizing the inanimate. We have as much right to do this as when we recognize that every existent reveals to the mind its form and essence.

There is purpose in every existent. Within purpose is its will to be recognized (known) for what it is and means. This comes to the existent during the process of creation; the intention of existence is found in its cause.

These are things which must be remembered if the epistemologist is to recognize his responsibility in defining the relationship between subject and object, and come to know when learning takes place. To answer the question,

What is cause? is to be aware of the empirical implications of the question, What does it mean to be causally effective?

When we ask this question, we cannot escape the need to define the relationship between will and cause. We shall define this relationship, (and also in the process, define cause) by stating a number of propositions.

First. While we have posited the belief that every existent exists because it was caused, our emphasis now is to be placed on the further belief that all human actions are caused. The argument is often heard that human action is caused only when such actions are in some way abnormal—when, for example, they are involuntary or irrational. This argument only begs the question; even involuntary or irrational arguments possess cause; since there is action, cause exists. If the action is caused by an irrational or involuntary means, this is but another condition upon which the mind must work.

Within the essence of cause lies reason and intent. The task of the mind is to discover the meaning (to learn) which cause intends in what is now the object of the cognitive process. The mind never asks for causes; that cause exists for all things is an assumption upon which the mind operates. To perceive cause in an existent is the beginning of the process of conceptualization so important to the functional capacity of the mind. It is the condition which cause has become, as the mind sharpens its perceptive eyes, which makes the mind operative. To make cause intelligible is to perceive it as the starting point of the intellective process. To be able to explain an object implies that the mind has experienced meaning; meaning will not be found in an object until its cause is explained. The answer to the question, What is its essence? can be found only in the mind's ability to actualize for itself the explanation resident in essence. What exists remains unknown until its cause explains its essence and purpose. To learn is to have experienced the meaning of essence by allowing cause to explain its intent. This is done by means of the subject in relation to its object. Cause does not possess mind, but the mind of First Cause gave to it purpose, a characteristic of all existence. In purpose resides all the empirical ingredients necessary for the cognitive process, what cause intends to reveal about itself.

Second. We could not take the foregoing position if we did not believe that cause is dependent upon First Principles. We have said that cause is dependent upon the human mind for the actualization of its potential. This is certainly a reference point in our consideration of the responsibility of the will in the learning process. But here we are talking about something quite different.

Cause is a part of created order. As such, it has its built-in systems which assures it that its essence possesses meaning. Because of its nature (form and essence) it reveals to the mind, when the mind has readied itself, its meaning. When this happens, object has become "one-with" the subject, and learning takes place.

First Cause, as Creator, in the process of creation, instilled First Principles in all existence. What was created as cause is now permitted to serve as the source of further creation, namely, what the mind creates from its objects.

What great difference there is in this position and that held by Hume when he would have us believe that the occurrence of the cause cannot entail the occurrence of anything else! This is the whole intent of cause!

Third. It is will that brings the mind into position to act. But only after the cognitive process has found the intended value implanted in the cause of an object, value validated, and the decision made. The mind now says, I am experiencing its meaning; it is purposeful for me, because . . . Here is an action, considered as movement, which is rapidly becoming the knowing process. In the knowing process, cause becomes internalized; this is what we mean by the mind being causally effective.

It should be apparent that our position implies that reason resides in cause, the rationality being the essence of cause itself. The teleological element is a characteristic of everything created; with the exception of First Cause, cause lies within the realm of the created. In this way, we can rightfully say that even giving a reason, reason here serving as cause, is in good epistemological order. However, we must not allow this thinking to cloud the distinctions we make between cause and reasons. Such a distinction is important to our entire epistemological schemata.

All of this leads us to draw at least one conclusion, namely, cause does not necessarily require the presence of a functional act which is purely physical in nature, to serve as its essence or the purport of its being. Cause functions according to its essence whether or not it be in keeping with the reasons for its existence or by the presence of its essence. That is, what it purports, or what it is able to do as a functional act. This means, reasons can serve to will change, but only when the reasons have been cognized and determined valid by the mind. It is in this way that the mind is caused to function. Here is another illustration of what it is that brings the causal condition into being. It is the mind, by means of its intellective process, which makes rationally effective the reason inherent in cause. The mind wills to act when its processes validate the reasons for movement. When the mind wills to act, it is always in a causally determined, therefore, effective way. To suggest that this position borders on a tautology is to fail to understand that the mind wills to act only on grounds empirical to the extent that they permit the mind to believe in what it is doing. Even when the time comes for the mind to make a value judgment, the empirical ground of its being must be satisfied. This is to say the mind always moves from an empirical base, which means nothing more than there is a demand to know the reason(s) in cause and its antecedents. This tells us that it is the empirical dimension of the cognitive process which is demanding to know why a cause is. Now we have come full circle in our question about reason(s) and cause. Thus, is the mind permitted to ask itself, Why do I believe as I do? It is reason in cause which forces consciousness to demand of mind and its processes to internalize the essence of the object being learned. It is cause which thereby determines whether what is being learned possesses an essence suggestive of something that can become productive. Learning is productivity; it is freeing the mind from its unknowing state; it is finding reason in what exists; freedom exists only in relation to what is known. This is what Plato meant when he said that we are free only when we are governed by reason. Before reason becomes part of the minds' processes, it must be known in cause. This I take as the meaning of Aristotle when he speaks of the relationship between reason and irrational feelings, and the actions which happen as a result of the relationship. Reason here must be considered as the essence of cause.

The freedom to will then, is to be found in the totality of cause, the being of reason. The being of reason is the need to establish the logical connectives between cause and effect by determining the epistemological relationship between necessity and what becomes reality through the process of knowing.

We cannot speak of reason in cause without considering the presence of logicality in the foremost characteristic of reason, namely, necessity. An existent is; but it implies something more than what the ontological proposition suggests. What is needed for the object to exist, is by reason of its essence, the *what* of necessity. Cause predicates nesessity; there is a relation to movement which the mind knows it cannot ignore. Necessity imposes upon the intellective process the epistemological weight in the confrontational relationship between subject and object, as subject considers the implications of constraining conditions which define the limitations found in reason. To even suggest then, that determining causes do not exist, is far from reasonable. Until the mind experiences reason in cause, it has not begun knowing by means of the intellective process, nor has the will become operational.

When the mind experiences reason in cause, I call causality. However, I am not thinking of the when in its chronological sense, that is, the point at which meaning is derived in the intellective process. Process is a developmental thing, in the same way we experience experience. Rather, I am using it in the Aristotlean sense, the mind, under necessity by reason in cause, now recognizes that if it is to learn, it has no alternative, it cannot do otherwise. This should clarify our intention above with respect to determining causes; cause is never static; while by its reason it has been determined; this state exists only for one purpose, namely, so it can caution one to determine; cause now becomes a part of the intellective process. Since process connotes movement, here is the point at which it is initiated.

Causality, will and their empirical relationship must then be defined in terms of the foremost characteristic of reason, necessity. Necessity is a characteristic of the moral as well as the physical world. In a sense, we refuse to distinguish between the two. The physical world too, by reason of purpose in cause, indicates a deep imprint of the moral. In this sense, there is a natural necessity found in every existent, regardless of form or essence. Perhaps this is what Kant was suggesting when he said that the rational being "can justly say of every unlawful action that he performs, that he could very well have left it undone; although as appearance it is sufficiently determined in the past, and in this respect is absolutely necessary."

Or, is he saying that perchance we should be aware of certain limitations of causality that are not present in cause?

Let us pick up that thought for just a moment. We offer the thesis that whatever limitation exists, it must be in reference to causality rather than to cause. We suggest the applicability of this thesis even though we are aware of the fact that when we proffered the basic idea of reason in cause, limitations would be a consideration, not in reference to cause, but rather to reason.

There are no limitations to cause because there are no limitations to First Principles or First Cause. This premise is based on the belief that all cause is psychologically initiated, unimpaired by mechanical accoutrements. Cause makes the distinction between physical or mechanical causality, and the psychologically based premise inherent in a determined teleology. Explanation for cause and its intention lies in its psychological stance alone, in what mind comes to know because of what it already knows. Here is another example of what we mean by the idea of necessity in condition. Limitations are governed by intention, the necessary conditions to essence in existence. It is causality which evidences cognitive concern (the need to identify) the limitations inherent in its responsibility to existing externals.

This means one thing; events are predictable when the mind knows the reason in cause; events (often purely physical) are unpredictable when the mind is unable to cognize the reason in cause; here is the cloud of unknowing. But all of this does not change our basic position, namely, events are, on principle, predictable. The point of emphasis here is on the word principle. When the principles inherent in reason in cause are understood, knowing happens and events become predictable. Every event has determining causes; the question of causality and predictability are then one and the same. This argument eliminates any thought that an event then, might be at random.

Cause possesses, as a part of its being, antecedents. It is the nature of cause to be its reason; it is this reason which serves as the internalized motivation for the intellective process to act.

When do we possess knowledge of antecedents? Since knowledge is essence in the process of becoming, we possess some knowledge of antecedents the moment we begin to take alternatives and conditions into consideration. All of this is necessary before a choice can be made and an act completed (in the incomplete sense). When the choice has been made and the act finalized, it is at this point in the process that the antecedents can be given their true evaluation and seen in the perspective of each relationship engendered. It is only in the context of these relationships that the meaningfulness of an antecedent can be actualized. There is, of course, no knowledge of an antecedent without knowing its meaningfulness to the intellective process.

Antecedents reside in cause. They serve as reasons for being of a particular object. Antecedents speak of principles which have been activated by the teleology in cause; they are what makes it possible for something else to be. They tell us that in the realm of the caused (that which exists because of First Cause) there are no entities. Whatever exists because something else has made it possible for it to exist. These are antecedents. Our knowledge of them came only by means of the intellective process.

How do we make a decision? At what point do we make the decision? What is the relationship between possible alternatives and the need to make a decision?

These are important questions, each of which must be answered if we are to understand the relationship between alternatives and the human will. To answer them, we use a reference point.

I have decided to attend a travelogue this evening. The decision has been made to go. So, I know what I intend to do. Moreover, I shall make every effort to be in my reserved seat before the film begins. Now, it would be out of place epistemologically speaking, if I were to say at this point that I am in the process of making up my mind whether or not to attend the showing of the film. By being out of place I mean this is not the place in the decision process for a consideration of alternatives. Alternatives force us back to an earlier point in the process. When I made the decision to go, I had already considered alternatives such as remaining home and working in my study or visiting with friends. Moreover, I knew that I intended to go, because I wanted to, more so than studying or visiting.

Alternatives are considerations before decisions are made. Whatever the process of decision, while I knew I intended to go, alternatives could have replaced the original intention. Knowledge of intention is limited to the intent, not to the decision itself. My decision could have been quite different.

How do we understand then, the process of decision? Perhaps the question should be asked differently. Did I know what I would finally decide to do? No, of course not. Knowledge would become complete only when the decision was made because the alternatives were considered. On the one side of alternatives is the problem of uncertainty. Until I decide if I should choose an alternative, my knowledge is incomplete and I am uncertain as to outcome. To make a decision about alternatives is to make the decision whether or not to attend the film. The certainty of knowledge comes with the decision. We must say then, that every decision is caused. But, just as important, it is necessary to say that every decision is a matter of choice.

The self-determined mind is free to make choices, that is, the choice between alternatives which the mind has validated. With the freedom to choose, the mind was free to select from among a number of alternatives but, the one chosen was given top priority for whatever reasons the mind justified as being valid.

This evening I have three alternatives, one of which is to attend the travel film, the one which I prefer and intend to choose. The other two, study or visiting, are also possible. I am determined to do one of the three; the one I choose will be my preference, because . . .

I am free to select any one of the three. Now, I would not be free if I have a lecture to deliver tomorrow for which I have not prepared. If I am to meet my lecture obligation (responsibility) then, I must study. Does this mean that I am not free because of the need to study for the lecture? Here, again, we must look at cause and responsibility. Since we believe that freedom of choice is always in relation to responsibility (and this is always in relation to alternatives) does this destroy the meaningfulness of the self-determined mind? No. I can still attend the film in spite of the lecture responsibility and pay the consequences. But because my mind is self-determined, the self being a responsible determiner, the other alternatives, visiting and going to the film, are not valid.

In the self-determined mind, responsibility is always a determiner; it is what makes the decision of the mind the resultant of what is logically (based on the reason in cause) necessary.

Condition

To determine logicality is to be aware of those conditions which will affect performance. If it is impossible to complete an intended action, conditions exist which prohibit completion. To know what these conditions are, and their nature, as well as the steps necessary to remove them, is the task of epistemology. It is clear enough to see that if the conditions did not exist, and since the action was willed, it is not the will which was stopped, but rather the action, and this, according to will, only temporarily. This is true only if the action would have resulted in producing something of value for the mind.

Conditions, when analyzed by the intellect, serve as yet other obstacles for the will to overcome. This is to say, conditions now become cause; something is going to be done because of their existence. Every action has at least an initiatory condition, which we call necessary. Action is both resultant and process. The will is concerned with both dimensions. An intended action is determined by condition and faced by potential conditions which may affect its completion. This is the most apparent characteristic of condition, that is, the consistency of its necessary relationships. This means that when I will an action, there are conditions which serve to initiate the action; there are also conditions which may attempt to hinder the action. It is the action which is hindered, not the will. The will never stops because of condition; it simply strengthens the hand of the intellect, and insists upon the need for more cognitive reinforcements. In spite of condition, the will is still willing to perform and complete its task. There is movement here that only the intellect can retard or stop. If the will is given to realize that there is now no value in the pursuit, it stops. Only in this way does the will maintain the integrity of its own nature.

This raises the question, Is condition a determinant? In a sense it is, but not in the way of suggesting that condition determines any thing else about the intellect other than forcing the intellect, because of the demands of the will, to act. The essence of the condition (what it is really saying) is simply providing the intellect with its task. The will says to the intellect, you must meet the conditions which confront us. I will provide the motivation. The real determinant in this case is found in the epistemological responsibility of the intellect. The need to meet the condition and solve its projections determines whether or not action will take place. The determined motive arises from within the intellect rather than from condition. This is what makes the intellection process self-determining in its methodology.

It should be remembered that condition makes it possible for the intellect to function. Since every action is caused, and underlying every cause is condition, we have condition to thank for providing us with the biography of the problem. Problems exist because of the conditions which first brought them into existence. It is well to remind ourself that learning takes place only in the presence of a problem. Condition, as a determinant, is responsible for bringing into being the self-determining process (known as the intellect) which alone can mean the difference between learning or only making a deposit in the brain bank.

To even suggest that such a condition as conditional certainty exists seems no more than a paradox, a play on words which were never meant for each other. Certainty precludes condition; condition implies question, something entirely out of place in the mind when the mind knows.

Knowledge is possessed when the mind has experienced its object; experience signals the recognition of meaning; meaning implies that certainty has been gained; the object has been fused with subject, and the truth inherent in what was object, is now possessed by the mind.

Certainty is the fringe benefit received together with knowledge. When one knows, the certainty of meaning is there as well. Otherwise, the possession is one of information, including facts known only as hypotheses, and data as indicators of potential knowledge. The fact loses its identity as a hypothesis when its essence has been experienced by the mind; fact then, becomes knowledge and its essence ascertained.

If conditions still exist, the intellective process has not completed its work. There is no certainty because knowledge is, as yet, incomplete.

What does certainty look like, then? The same as knowledge; and remember, for knowledge to exist, it must be able to experience its essence. It looks like this. There is no question in my mind, therefore, I possess this certainty: New York City is in the State of New York. First of all, I speak in terms of concepts, namely, New York City, not as a place, but as an idea. Since ideas depend on other ideas, and ideas learn from ideas, I know New York City in relation to many other things, such as other cities, the Atlantic Ocean, the eastern seaboard, the parameters of the State of New York, the State of New York in relation to surrounding states, etc.

Now, then, I must be careful to always protect myself in the knowing process, and I do this by way of qualification. Concepts permit us to do this. An example might be: I know that the City of New York is in New York state; I am now thinking of New York City as a place. But during the time I spend in writing this, a disaster could overtake the city, and it no longer exists. Here is qualification, because these conditions make my knowledge conditional, changing it to a hypothetical fact, and therefore, no longer certain.

Because all material of knowledge begins on the premise of condition, and, therefore, more rightfully must carry the data, the mind recognizes the need to look upon the material of data, not in isolation, but in relation to its many inevitable conditions.

Certainty is a mind-state, reached when mind experiences the experience of the totality of its knowledge. The mind has every intention of knowing fully its objects; certainty is gained by degrees, as knowledge increases, and, in the process, the mind apprehends the degrees of truth.

What does this say to the learner's freedom? If the learner acts because he is caused to act as he does by some antecedent, is he free? No, if he wills to be caused, he is not free. The causality inherent in physical force may not present a choice. Freedom, however, is always psychologically based; if the mind is not given the opportunity to choose, there is a different type of determination here which cannot be ignored. With chance comes the opportunity to do otherwise. The learner, by means of the intellective process, can become the cause of his own actions; in this sense he becomes cause; he may cause many different actions, all of which imply that they were caused.

In choice, the mind deliberates upon cause and its reasons. In this way it is actualizing its teleological needs. When it is able to validate reason in cause, it is ready to will action. It is will, then, which possesses a power of determination which includes freedom of choice in the mind which has accepted its responsibility to know by becoming cause.

Since it is our contention that the human mind basically is a self-determining construct, this might suggest that our position is this.

Chance is not "something" which may be the cause of a happening, nor is it a reality factor in what may happen as a reason in the learning process. This is not our position, for a number of reasons.

While I do believe that the human mind is a self-determining construct, this does not mean to imply that it always functions in this way. It is the will which is the determinant here; if the will is diseased, the chance is very great that the mind will never realize its potential in this area of its being. This tells us then, that the mind is often tempted to leave things to chance, those things which may happen as a result of a new set of relationships which have been formed.

Chance is another of the conditions which constantly confront the mind, and which may serve as a determinant in making of the mind something other than what it could will to become.

On the one hand you have the necessity factor inherent in the position of self-determinacy and, on the other, what we are tempted to call pure chance, yet hesitant to do so.

If by pure chance we mean what happens without reason and not possessing the teleological ingredient, our argument would stand without empirical grounds. In time, we may even assume the stand of asking if chance exists other than as a word. Or, when we study, in depth, the nature of a coincident, is the factor of necessity missing in a series of coincidences?

What really lies behind a happening, act or event? Chance? Or, the result of what was necessary to complete an act or action? Or, the conditions which underlie chance, is there, really a change in the nature of the confrontation facing the mind as a problem?

What I am requesting here is a consideration of this thought. Even among material things, the inanimate, is it possible for things to happen without the element of reason inherent in cause? If this is true, chance is but a word.

It is not necessity which gives rise to epistemological inevitability, but chance; if we discredit the whole idea of chance, then we make it possible to recognize an inevitability of a different stripe to exist, now in relation to necessity. What is self-determined leaves nothing to chance, and the element of inevitability is recognized as a cognitive ingredient of the will.

In this conversion, it must be remembered that whatever the mind handles, has a history. Every idea, concept, thing or action writes its own autobiography in the process of its becoming known. As the mind comes to know, it moves in its relation to its own constructs as these are writing the biography of the problem (e.g. the idea). In this way, the historical process is an integral part of the intellective process. There is no such a thing as a non-historical factor relating to a thing or concept.

All of this forces the mind back to cause. What exists can never be known in isolation. This premise is based on the belief that when there is an existent, it exists only because something else exists; the word entity is much like the word chance. As words they exist, but anything more than this?

Since events have conditions, is there room for chance?

The necessity factor in self-determinism is always a historical determinism. The fact that conditions exist is proof of this epistemological pudding. Cause often expresses itself in empirical chains, the chief characteristic of which is dependency upon the historicity of the directives for analysis found in every condition. This is the rational constituent in what carries its own teleological perspective, namely, the historical present. From what was, and now is, the mind is able to decide upon what is necessary to produce the possible, what can be known. Does it sound as though chance has a chance in such an epistemological schemata for knowing, or perhaps we should say, the willing to know? The mind balances effect, that is, knowing, with cause. Knowing is to produce an analysis of cause in terms of all of its historical components.

When it is functioning as a self-determining totality, the mind operates as an epistemological planner. In this capacity, it leaves nothing to chance. But, when it comes empirically lazy, and does not determine what happens as the intellective process functions, it may chance what otherwise would not come into being.

With respect to its object? What is out there to be known? Herein the nature of the problem changes, the historical circumstances being quite different.

As epistemological planner, the mind realizes it must strengthen its position with respect to the relationship between chance and cause. Again, we are confronted with the problem question, is there a chance ingredient in what is caused? To ask it in yet another way, is there such a thing as an accident? I contend that cause is always present in any act; however, it may not be the intended cause of the mind.

My son and I are playing catchball. The plan is a simple one. The ball is thrown back and forth; we hope to catch it each time it is thrown. The mind intends, because it is willed, that the ball is thrown so that it can be caught. As the ball leaves my hand, a strong wind drives the ball from the intended path, and instead of catching the ball, my son is struck by it. My intention was not that the ball strike my son. It was an accident, you say. But what happened had a cause, the wind. Was it by chance that the wind blew at that particular speed and at that specific spot? We would have to say that there is a condition which perhaps I should have taken into consideration. But how did I know the wind would blow at that moment? Perhaps it was a chance the mind was taking when it declared its intention? Is cause then, in this connection, always external to the mind? Is the mind entitled to say, my responsibility ends when it has declared its intentionality?

There is nothing of the accident sense about intention. There is, of course, in relation to a completed act. However, if I choose to act, it is because I intend it, and there is nothing accidental about this. This puts us in complete disagreement with Ayer. Choosing is an act of mind; accidents happen to things other than the mind, with this one qualification, unless it is to the unwilled mind, the disordered mind.

The element of choice is purposive and teleological in nature. When I choose, I do so with some purpose and end in mind; if what I choose is not what I get, this does not mean that I choose by accident. The accident arises from a lack of knowledge in the process of intending. Here is another way to look upon the relationship between chance and cause.

Responsibility of the mind in its intellective process is always determined by its relationship to decision; intending it is a question of degree. Our conclusion at this point in our discussion must be: but what about the absence of cause? For things outside the mind? Impossible. For things thought of as mind? Impossible. Whatever exists (with the exception of First Principle) exists because there is cause.

The mind disclaims responsibility in the acts of those things over which it has no control; the mind actively engaged in its epistemological function of willing, accepts the responsibility of implementing intention. This the cognitive process. It is not a process run on chance.

Of course things happen in the universe over which the mind has no control, and which the mind is unable to predict; but it is the mind which says, if I possessed the knowledge of why they happened, would I be inclined to say, they happened by chance?

This confronts us with this kind of question, is this a deterministic universe in which we live? And, is the mind made of the same stuff as the universe, and therefore deterministic, as well? We have answered the question above and certainly have made it clear that the mind, while it can allow itself to be determined, according to the nature of its being, is the self-determining construct of the personal human self.

We agree with Campbell that "man cannot be morally responsible for an act which does not express his own choice but is, on the contrary, attributable to chance." We must qualify what we mean by chance; while it was chance (in only one sense of the word) that the ball hit my son, even chance has a cause, which changes its nature almost completely. Perhaps we should search for a better word.

The learner is someone who is acted upon; he is in the process of knowing how, when and why this is happening; but he is also one who acts because he is free to determine (cause) what now becomes caused. Perhaps we are free then to add to one of Hobbes' statements: nothing takes a beginning from itself—except First Cause—all things possess antecedents in their reason for being.

Without faith in the purity of reason in First Cause, the mind can never become conscious of its freedom to will, and to do so by becoming a self-determiner.

What It Means to be Conscious of Freedom

When we speak about an acting being, the question of cause is raised; there is an objectivity about this which is just as true as when we speak of the acting mind. Since mind requires a referrant in order to function, and one of the operational principles is constantly at work cognizing the objective essence of cause in order to confront consciousness with the negatives inherent in condition, it remains for the mind to move from its involvement in negatives to the discoveries characteristic of positives. It should not be forgotten that Hegel was not hesitant to suggest that the mind is the negative. Our explanation of this rests upon the assumption that the mind is what it purports, but the *is* becomes by means of consciousness, the cognizing dimension of perception. The edge of consciousness is sharpened by the mind's need for an awareness of all conditions and their implications which pertain to a given problem. The ability to perceive is achieved by the transparency factor brought into being by the cognitive scapel of consciousness, namely, awareness. In the intellective process, it is awareness and its attributes which accepts the responsibility for providing direction to the intellective process. It is in this way that consciousness becomes aware of the history and biographical components of an idea. It is not the task of consciousness to posit the end or goal for the process to function; it is consciousness which is aware of what the process must accomplish if knowledge is to be gained; in this way, mind is enabled to experience its object and learn.

The subject of awareness and its consideration as being, the being of consciousness, must be looked at in terms of its relationship to consciousness. Because it is the being of consciousness, consciousness is dependent upon the chief characteristic of awareness, namely, its directive contextual powers, for the heightening of its own motivation. This means that with awareness, there is awareness of something; consciousness now has direction and what it is aware of, is seen in context. Awareness puts the things of the mind (its essence) in proper perspective; one existent is seen in relation to another existent, and both are seen in terms of dependency relationships.

Consciousness does not depend upon the traits of awareness to provide it with knowledge. Awareness is the type of functional activity which surfaces on both ends of the learning continuum. While awareness heightens the alertness quality of consciousness, thereby alerting the mind to the potentiality of an object for knowing, it also appears in its advanced degrees of apprehension because the mind knows, its ability for greater and greater awareness soon makes itself evident.

There is then, awareness of potentialities in an object under learning scrutiny, as well as awareness of yet greater yields in an act in the process of being completed.

Consciousness feeds on the content of consciousness; its means is provided by awareness and its dependency upon the intellective process.

Consciousness then, is an active agent in the learning process. Its past does not act upon it; rather, it acts upon its own history and refuses to believe that its essence comprises but a chain of events. It is a self-directed activity, not determined, a self-determining mind-action, governing the nature of the methodology to be used by the intellect. It is a mind-factor which refuses to even suggest accommodation or adjustment to condition or question; it is the lead horse, so to speak, in the mind's movement toward knowing. Thoroughness in perception is a chief characteristic; certainty in knowledge is its goal.

The mind refuses to separate consciousness from its activity; activity would be meaningless without it. Moreover, the mind is aware of its need for consciousness in order to understand itself, its essence and methodologies.

In part, all of this is a matter of identity. I speak of the mind's dependency on the ability of consciousness to forge its own powers of intensity. This forces us to take a look at the essence of consciousness. What is it, really?

We would make quite a mistake if we would equate consciousness with states of awareness rather than states of consciousness. It is awareness which develops by fusing states because of its perceptive abilities of apprehension. To speak of the states of consciousness is to place a limitation upon its responsibility to all facets of the intellective process.

It is consciousness which provides the intellective process with the determinant for making the decision as to the needed intensity of process to achieve understanding beyond the knowledge of ascertained facts. Thus, the identity factor becomes the mode for identifying at what stage of the scientific method the intellect is to begin its search for knowledge, and the depth of analysis necessary to accomplish its task.

At each step of the process of knowing, the intellect will be confronted by the conditions of the object being studied. Awareness of the implications of those conditions makes it possible for the mind to move step by step in its analysis; it is consciousness which looks upon the condition as a positive means whereby further knowledge is experienced. It is consciousness which possesses the epistemological perspective of the learning process.

Consciousness is the one factor which keeps the intellective process from becoming discouraged in its search for knowledge. Consciousness alerts the intellect to its own stance: as long as conditions exist, there is more to know about the object; the fact remains, as yet, a hypothesis. In this sense, consciousness is the totality which assures the mind of continued action; there are always new relationships to be found among existents. It is consciousness which provides the opportunities for the mind to become creative in methodology and perspective. Essentially, it is what consciousness demands of the intellect, namely, that it becomes an intellective process. When I speak of opportunities I am thinking of what is provided by consciousness for the intellect. It is not a characteristic of consciousness to tell the intellect; rather, it (consciousness) moves by means of the opportunities, that is, the ideas which are constantly being proferred, which permit the intellect to move from positions of strength, and not of weakness, as Popper suggests. This is one more indication of the intent of consciousness to assure movement by the intellective process of the mind.

The foregoing premises force us into the position of saying, the mind does not possess consciousness, it is consciousness. Consciousness makes it possible for the mind to do what it does by means of its processes.

When mind is conceived of as consciousness it is then aware of its epistemological responsibilities to itself. It is consciousness which makes every action of the mind intentional, therefore, self-determining. For those who inquire about the place of the unconscious at this point, it is sufficient to say, the unconscious, without a doubt, plays a large part in the intellective process; the unconscious, however, is a meaningless factor in the knowing process until its essence is cognized, therefore, made a part of consciousness. We cannot suggest that unintentionality is a characteristic of the unconscious; unintentionality does not exist in the intellective process. All consciousness portends intentionality.

Mind, in moving through and by means of its intellective process, places before itself, in its total consciousness, the condition of awareness; without it, the mind does not move and its functionaries, such as the factor of cognition, are not operative. There is action only when there is consciousness. Thinking takes place only because consciousness produces the intellectual setting in which this function now is enabled to conceptualize. It is consciousness which demands of the thought process the need to conceptualize. Without conceptualizing, thought remains but a process reviewing hypotheses.

Because of consciousness, the mind is aware of what it is doing; it is aware of the fact that it is acting, and why it is acting as it does by means of the chosen functionaries of the intellective process. The language of consciousness permits this dialogue, (bringing into being this awareness) to actualize itself as ends in mind, in the sense that Wittgenstein uses the idea of acquisition—the mind justifying what it possesses by means of knowing why the knowledge has meaning. This is why, in our first sentence about consciousness, we said, when we speak about an acting being, the question of cause is raised.

To this relationship I now have an obligation. When I fulfill the obligation, I am acting responsibly. What is my obligation? To be present for the tutorial and meet the goals mutually determined in this particular learning setting.

Now then, I am under obligation to be present at 2 p.m. For the sake of discussion, we make two quite different hypotheses.

Conditions have changed. I now find it impossible to be present. We must ask the question, Why? Because on my way to the tutorial, on leaving the library, I tripped on one of the steps, and must be taken to the hospital. There is no way for me to be present at the tutorial. Am I now still under obligation to be present? Conditions have made it impossible; am I acting irresponsibly? Hardly, unless I fail to send word to my student to explain what has happened, since it is possible for me to send such a message. The contract, as such, has not been broken, nor has the obligation lessened in its meaningfulness.

However, I find myself comfortably settled at my writing desk working with a great deal of ease doing what I greatly enjoy, writing. My mind is functioning in a way which pleases me; the thoughts come much more rapidly than I can put down on paper. I look at my watch and see that I have only five minutes to cross campus to my office and the tutorial.

Something happens. I begin to rationalize. I begin to tell myself things are going so well here; if I stopped writing, it would be so difficult to pick up my thoughts at a later time. Perhaps the student is not prepared, or he would appreciate more time to think through his approach; perhaps he is tired and needs a break because, after all, we have been meeting every week for many months, etc.

Shades of delusion! What is the mind doing? What is the will permitting to happen? Am I acting responsibly? Am I not under obligation to be present, in spite of what I am telling myself? What does this reaction tell me about myself in relation to an obligation?

What am I allowing to happen? If I follow this line of supposed reason I am permitting these rationalizations to determine (and change) my relationship to an obligation. On the other hand, if I am able to reason (to see reason in cause) rather than rationalize (with all of its weaknesses) I will validate the real reasons in cause and on this basis draw a conclusion in relation to what is the greatest good for that particular obligation.

We have two settings. First, I am injured and have been taken to the hospital; there is no possible way for me to fulfill the contractural obligations at the moment. However, I can make a phone call and explain my absence, thereby fulfilling the spirit of the obligation. Second, even though I recognize the validity of remaining at my writing desk, because of writing conditions, this is not sufficient cause for me not to meet my obligation because the greatest good would be for me and not for the particular obligation.

Intention finds its source of motivation in cause; in cause lies the *a priori* argument demanding the need to cognize assumptions. Consciousness is constantly reminding the mind and its processes of its need to handle the problem of intention in every presupposition. Here is the means chosen by consciousness to make certain that causal efficacy is not forgotten by the intellect in its process of movement toward knowing.

The mind will never will unless it is conscious of its freedom to do so. What is the setting on which this consciousness comes into being? In its relationship to First Cause; in this relationship the mind learns that First Cause intends that the human mind should become a self-actualizer, the process of which includes the need to determine the nature of its own value system. The purity of reason in First Cause includes, in its projected opportunities for knowing an existent, the means by which the human mind can develop its own methodology for learning. Faced with the opportunity for knowing, the mind must determine its methodology for learning. The first step in this process means possessing the awareness of a basic freedom to learn.

It is in cause and its reasons for existence the openness to opportunities for learning is found. The question, what are the possibilities for knowing? since I now possess the freedom to learn, is in order.

The Relationship between Freedom and Knowledge

What is this relationship? What am I free to know? An answer which carries its own logicality is, Whatever is potentially knowable. We might explain this by saying there are specifics which are, quite literally, unknowable, like the essence of the being of the Absolute. How can a non-absolute know that which is Absolute? If this were possible, the non-absolute would be a non-existent. What is knowable also provided the freedom to be known if the human mind is open because it has become a self-determiner and uses an adequate methodology for learning. I am not free to know all there is to know about the sun; the potentiality is not there for knowing because of what (the essence) the sun is (its condition, one of which is the heat factor) and secondly, I am not equipped, academically to handle the epistemological problems, namely, my responsibility for bringing the knowledge into being.

What about the knowledge upon which I base a prediction? I am certainly free to make a prediction with the knowledge I now possess. This morning at eight, I met one of my students, registered in my eleven o'clock class, on the steps of the library and said to him, I'll see you in class. I, then, proceeded to my writing desk in the library. I did not know at eight that at ten I would be called to a meeting making it impossible to lecture at eleven, consequently, breaking the prediction of seeing the student in class. Because of the nature of the meeting and the responsibility involved, a value judgment was made upon the value conditions, and I was no longer free to keep my commitment. It must be remembered the prediction was made under different conditions;

a new alternative was now advanced, the nature of which completely changed the nature of freedom and its implications. This is not to say that I was not free to attend class; I could have willed such action; however, the nature of freedom changes since the mind wills its own freedom. I now needed the freedom to attend the meeting which I decided was more important than the class. If choices are irrevocable, then objects become determinants which leave no opportunity for choice. If I say I have no choice but to lecture, even in the face of conditions which change my relationship to the lecture, the mind is no longer a self determiner and a free agent.

If I have no choice but to lecture, or, I have no choice but to attend the meeting, what is it that forces me to make a decision, one way or another? What is the basic upon which I make a value judgment? Do I not move from a moral premise? Is it not from this moral premise that I derive my freedom? A freedom which assures me I have met my obligations?

As soon as the word responsibility has been uttered, the agent is aware of a lingering taste of another word, another implication, namely, obligation. Like responsibility, obligation is a concept, and must be seen as such in any analysis of the nature of the human will. While the epistemologist finds these words having quite different meanings, they are intimately related; their individual and separate value lies wholly in the nature of their relationship. The mind is quite aware of the fact that it does not know responsibility until it has validated its obligations; the moment obligations are considered by way of their implications, this consideration in itself is indicative that the problem of responsibility is being evaluated.

What then, is obligation considered by the mind as a concept? We move toward a definition.

As I scan my daily calendar I note a tutorial scheduled for 2 p.m. This is a regularly scheduled session with one of my doctoral candidates. In preparation, specific readings were assigned and the writing of a position paper. He has informed me that he will be present and, at the moment, I see no reason why I cannot be in my office at that time.

As we move into this study, there are a number of assumptions we bring with us. First, there is an agreement between student and tutor that a minimum number of sessions will be held; moreover, that a specific subject will be covered in the tutorial, and a certain number of books researched and papers written. Second, because of the nature of the relationship, each of us has entered upon it with a mature sense of responsibility.

When I say that I will validate the real reasons in cause and on this basis draw a conclusion in relation to what is the greatest good for that particular obligation, I am speaking of judgments in relation to the concept of obligation. The moment the mind is concerned with validity, the value condition and value judgment are brought into focus. Such a stance is determined by my use of the will in the degree to which the real reasons in cause are actualized. It may be nothing more than the psychological build-up which now says, I really don't want to go to the tutorial; my writing is moving too smoothly, and I would much rather write than listen to the reading of a position paper and discuss its content. This may be the real reason why I do not go to the tutorial; the conditions have made the setting and fostered the attitudinal stances. However, the real question has not been raised. While I recognize and accept the value of the writing conditions, the value judgment is saying two things: first, the tutorial condition is not being considered. Because he is a conscientious student, there is no question but his position paper is ready for reading, and the opportunity for its analysis will be there; second, the decision is mine, and it is couched in the question of ought. It is possible for me to be present (I can); now, ought I? It is here the morality of the relationship takes on meaning.

What we are asking is really this, Is there a morality inherent in every obligation? And our answer is, Yes, of course. It must be remembered that as the agent in this case, I am merely obligated because of the existence of free choice. If the validation process is a true one, and the mind is permitted to act responsibly, it will draw a positive and affirmative relation to what is the greatest good for that particular obligation. In other words, with a great deal of haste I make my way to the tutorial.

The word obligation is interesting; it has the potentiality for getting us into a pack of epistemological trouble. This is quickly seen as we now return to an earlier example, in the fact that I have an obligation to my class to lecture at eleven. I have contracted with my students and therefore am under obligation to meet the terms of the agreement. If I do not lecture and yet was free to do so, the contract has been broken. But, am I free when my mind has determined the need to fulfill a more important obligation? The mind has replied by using (instead of making) a value judgment. Essentially it was a judgment of "obligability." Within the value judgment resides the means whereby it justifies its own actions. Again, unless the mind has this freedom, it is not a self-determiner. Unless the mind has this freedom, it cannot make (because it now uses) the value judgment and do so within the context of its sense of self-correcting responsibility. It is only the mind which can be held accountable for self-correcting action. The question, Is the mind acting responsibly? is the same as asking, Is the mind working from a moral premise already validated?

Another question is in order. Would the mind even bother to use a value judgment if it did not move on the reason which is inherent in the moral premise? If the mind is free to will to know, this freedom is guaranteed only because of the reason inherent in the moral premise. The value judgment moves from the base of this reason which says, it is necessary to go to the meeting, instead of the lecture, because . . . A conclusion has been reached on the basis of reason and for reasons now validated. When a value judgment is used, the mind is using, freely, the morality inherent in reason. Without this morality, the mind would not know it was free to even use the value judgment. This, in one sense, is what Kant is speaking about when he would have us remember there is a causality which is capable of spontaneously originating a series of events. These are the events which ultimately took me to the meeting rather than to the lecture.

While Kant speaks of a series of events, I speak of a process which took me to the meeting. Moreover, I went quite spontaneously, not because I did not want to lecture but rather, because I was compelled (in the good sense) by the inherent responsibility, to do what was most important. This is the whole purpose of using the value judgment as the means by which the moral premise is actualized. This compulsion does not affect freedom; it is related not to freedom but to the will. Whenever I will, the totality of the mind is literally compelling itself to act; the self is now in psychological movement. Too many epistemologists make the mistake of believing that compulsion is a problem. Of course it is a problem for the determined mind; but then, the determined mind is not free, and whatever is determined is under compulsion to act because it is being caused; no psychological brakes are being applied because the mind has decided to will passivity.

Because of its processes, the self-determined mind decides to act, and because it has decided that the object of its action will bring good into being, it compels itself to act; the outcome of the willing process is action. This compulsion, is it the result of the law of cause and effect? To ask the question in another way, is the self-determined mind subject to the law of cause and effect or, the subject which makes the law of cause and effect meaningful? Without question, it is the latter. The compulsion problem is not a problem for the self-determined mind.

There is no Conflict between Freedom and Nature

Of the many epistemologists who speak of the relationship between freedom and nature, St. Thomas provides us with the means whereby it is possible to severely limit the scope of the problem. His argument is clear and concise.

He tells us: It is contrary to the whole concept of liberty that what is free should be the first cause of itself.

The key idea here evolves from the words *first cause*. These words change the nature of the free-will controversy because the freedom of the will finds itself as an operant only when the mind functions as second cause. That is, the mind wills its own freedom. In order to do this it must function as second cause. However, this does not detract from St. Thomas' position when he says that not only is God the ultimate cause of what a man freely chooses to do, as He is the First Cause of every natural event, but the will as a natural faculty never moves itself to operation. It is always moved by the reason, even in its acts of choice, and so these acts, wherein the will is free, are also cause.

Aquinas here speaks of God as Absolute and First Cause. This presents us with no problem. This Absolute is also the first cause of every natural event. To this we must not react too hastily. What he means is that as "First Cause" there is reason (which carries its own logicality) for whatever happens. This reason is *in* Cause; in one sense, it *is* Cause. As cause, by means of its reason(s), it literally projects purpose and, in purpose, meaning.

We now come to a most salient point. The will as a natural faculty of man (as one of the three domains of the function mind, namely, the affective, cognitive, and conative) never moves itself to operation. It always moves itself by the reason, that is, which is inherent in First Cause. The will never moves solely. It functions only by means of its dependency relationship with the two other domains of the mind. In other words, there is the Reason of the Absolute as First Cause, and there is the reason as the total function of the human mind.

Aquinas is an alert epistemologist; whereas he may feel comfortable with the position stated above, he knows only too well it is far from complete.

He tells us: Like Augustine, a distinction must be made between those acts of the will which are necessitated and those which are free. However, natural necessity does not take away the liberty of the will. That liberty exists only in "the will's choice of means, not in its validation of the end."

Of course there is necessity expressed in purpose and meaning. Necessity always exists where Mind (absolute) has reasoned. Necessity is the conceptual connective in all true logic, the expression of the law of sequence. Augustine and Aquinas are speaking of a natural necessity; we call the attention of the reader to their emphasis upon the word natural. It is natural because it has been reasoned by First Cause. There is a second point of emphasis, namely, this natural necessity does not take away the liberty of the will. The liberty or freedom is the freedom willed by the mind free to choose means. That is, the mind confronted by acts of natural necessity which have implications for the totality of that same mind.

He tells us: There is also a naturalness and necessity about the will in its relationship to the affective and cognitive domains of the mind. Just as the will is always moved by the reason, the reason, that is, of First Cause, and never moves on its own powers of volition, it is well to remember, he says, the intellect (the three domains of the mind) naturally and of necessity adheres to First Principles, so the will adheres to the last end.

Another point in our favor, he reminds us is, just as the intellect assents of necessity to those

> propositions which have a necessary connection with first principles,
> namely demonstrable conclusions, . . . so the will adheres of necessity

only to those things . . . which have a necessary connection with happiness.

The conclusion to which he brings us then, is this: the will itself is not necessitated, and so its choice among means is free.

Hume on Necessity

This brief review of the thinking of Aquinas on the subject of freedom and motive, with particular emphasis on the question of necessity, leaves us with a few lingering problems, many of which Hume has considered and discussed. The thoughtful epistemologist does not forget the position of Hume on liberty. It is a significant statement and shades of its implications are seen on every page of this study.

Hume's stand is clear and concise, namely, men are free; moreover, all their actions are casually determined.

There is a starkness about these words. At face value they may be acceptable, that is, if one can live comfortably within paradox. Maybe what is needed is a qualifier. Is it logical to say in the same breath that while every action is causally determined, man is free? Seemingly, this is illogical, inconsistent, and paradoxical. Is it? Is there a qualifier? While we have already addressed ourselves to this problem, we now take the time to analyze Hume's position, since he says there is no "philosophical" problem of free will. Moreover, Hume does not greatly assist us to resolve it, other than confronting us with problem areas which cannot be ignored. Now if Hume is saying that if there is a problem, the problem itself is created by a mind which does not understand its own function, I would quite agree. But is this what he is saying?

Hume requires us to stop seven times on the pathway to an understanding of his position. At some points our stay will be short because we find no problem; at another point our lay-over will be long, for there is much to resolve.

1. Hume believes that "causation is essentially constant succession." While his discussions speak to this proposition, we question whether Hume has fully answered the question, what is causation? Moreover, I do not believe that he has satisfactorily answered the question, what is the source of, or reason behind, causation? Causation is not a given. If he is willing to equate First Cause and Causation, or even Second Cause and Causation, our problem is not particularly acute. What are the empirical premises upon which causation can be said to be essentially constant succession? To what must we attribute the power of causation if it is constant succession? This problem is compounded when we turn to the second step.

2. Hume believes there is no necessary connection between causes and their effects. Now, this is more than a semantical problem. If the word cause is used, it must mean what it implies, that it is the cause of something. If of

something, what? Something quite different from what it intends? That is, cause. Our problem begins with the word necessary. If there is no necessary connection between causes and their effects, before we raise other questions, the word 'their' confronts us. Again, we have a study in paradox.

What is he saying? There are causes which have no effects, and effects which are not caused? This is difficult to believe. Nevertheless, it is possible to interpret his statement in this way. Rather, before asking further questions, let us listen a third time.

3. Hume believes that causes "do not complete the occurrence of their effects they only precede them." Are we out of the woods? Hardly. We have only started to feel the effects of an epistemological anguish. This is a difficult proposition to interpret. We could go astray in our interpretation of his use of the word compel. If we equate this word with the idea of free, our trouble may be the same in nature. If there is no necessary connection between cause and effect why is it necessary to say there is no compelling of an occurrence in relation to effect? However, even the thought that cause precedes effect is in contradiction to what has been said above. Perhaps Hume will clarify the problem as we take the next step.

4. Hume believes that with respect to human actions, the question as to whether or not they are caused is, in reality, the question of "whether there is anything with which they are constantly joined." His explanation is this. "Throughout history certain actions have always been associated with certain motives with the same constancy and regularity that one finds between any causes and their effects." "Human actions are caused, then, in the same way that everything else is caused."

Here, again, the question is being begged. To say that the determinant which is the connective between cause and effect is the factor of being constantly joined by something, and using the word 'whether' to suggest that perhaps, at times, this is not the case, is to fail to understand the nature, scope and purpose of First Cause. If we recall an earlier premise which stipulates that the only existing entity is First Cause, and all else, as a part of a created order, exists only because something else exists, thereby giving to each existent a depending relationship to something else (which says, an existent exists because something else exists), we must say there is always that something which gains contantly existents. In other words, there is in all things an inherent relationship to other things. Cause and effect reside in the very nature of all existents. As reason is First Cause because it is in First Cause, cause and effect is made of the created order because it is in the created order.

5. Hume believes, as we said above, that human actions are free. Is this a logical conclusion in the light of what we have been discussing? We let him answer by retracing our thoughts two paragraphs when he said that throughout history certain actions have always been associated with certain

motives with the same constancy and regularity that one finds between any causes and their effects. What he is really saying is that it is in the very nature of a free action that it springs from "the motive of the agent." If he means that the mind because of its motives wills its own freedom, fine. That is, at least, in part. For here we must ask, what has validated the motives, and governed their "constancy and regularity"? Because the motive is constant and regular actually tells us very little about it.

This is suggestive that the mind has not been pre-determined, but, at least, in part, it is functioning as a self-determiner. If this is true, then our only problem becomes one of determining the validity of its motives. What compels the mind to act? This is a question which cannot be bypassed.

6. In his sixth statement, Hume tells us that freedom is being able to act according to the determination of one's own will. No doubt what he means is acting according to one's own motives, and not according to the motives of someone or something else.

What compels the mind to act? Motives, one's own. Our epistemological thirst remains unquenched.

7. Hume believes then, that "one's actions are not unfree if they are caused but if they are caused by something other than the determinations of one's own will." This seventh step has been taken even though it is a repeat step because of what is now being implied.

Let me react to all seven steps.

It is quite apparent that Hume believes his position does not detract from what he feels is the responsibility of the agent, namely, man is responsible for what he does. It requires an epistemological boldness to say this, but starkness is taken from the statement when the degree of emphasis Hume places upon motives is remembered. As we have suggested, Hume's key concept revolves about the motive; responsibility does depend upon the causation of actions by motives.

How does Hume arrive at this position? The answer to this question is quite simple when his assumptions are listed and carefully studied. They are as follows:

1. "All laws are based on rewards and punishments and thus rest on the assumption that mens' motives can be relied upon to have a regular influence on their behavior."

2. There would be no point in appealing to such practices as fear and hope if nothing could be predicted from their operation. Justice, moreover, requires such an operation of motives, for no man can be a fit object of punishment if his actions are in no way traceable to his motives.

3. ". . . if one could not rely upon the constant and predictable operation of motives, all intercourse with one's fellows would be hazardous or impossible."

He is, in a very real sense, confronting us with two problems, namely, determinism and prediction. This is what I mean.

It is safe to assume that a number of people will be killed by lightning sometime during the coming summer. How many of those people do you suppose expect to be killed by lightning sometime in the next few months? Probably no one has "reason to expect it." Add to this, how many of those people do you suppose would predict being killed by lightning sometime within the next few months? You ask, what is the difference between expectation and prediction? That is not the question to ask. Whether it is expectation or prediction, is it possible to even suggest that lightning has no cause?

"Determinism, then, does not imply that all human behavior is predictable in the most straight forward sense of the term, for many unpredictable things are nevertheless causally determined."

A few moments ago I attempted to push my chair away from the writing table. It would not move. I don't know why. It might be that I didn't push hard enough. Or, that an adhesive attached itself to the bottom of the chair when last I moved it, and since it has been in this position for sometime, and with the weight of my body upon it, it has glued itself to the floor. Or, as I now found out from experimenting, there is a small hole in the tile, and the leg is lodged in the hole and must be lifted out before it will move. Since I did not know about the hole, or the other possibilities, I had made no prediction about being unable to move the chair. The cause was there, but I did not know about it. Because the chair did not move, I supposed a cause.

For Hume, all of this is sufficient reasoning to say that while our actions may be caused, we are also free.

We still have not resolved the problem of the 'maybe' in relation to cause.

Wherein Lies Freedom?

We now shift our attention to a problem which requires as much attention as has been given to Hume. It is our contention that the mind possesses the ability to will its own freedom when it makes the decision to function as a self-determiner. There is a basic question here. Is the freedom in the mind to will its own freedom, or is the freedom in the will to decide to function as a self-determiner?

Why raise the question when will is an integral part of mind, and mind includes will as one of its domains? Is it because Descartes forces us to do so? We know where Descartes stands on the question. He places freedom in the will. Moreover, he identifies it with the power of choice.

He wishes to make three points. First, the faculty of will consists alone in having the power (that is, the agent as the one having the power) of choosing to do a thing or choosing not to do it. He writes: ". . . it consists alone in the fact that in order to affirm or deny, pursue or shun, those things placed before us by the understanding, we act so that we are unconscious that any outside force constrains us in so doing." Second, the will is the cause of itself as evidenced in its acts of choice. He writes: "The knowledge of the understanding should always precede the determination of the will." To this, he adds: "Our will impels us neither to follow after nor to be free from anything, except as our understanding represents it as good or evil."

His use of the word represent could throw us off the track of the question, wherein lies freedom? But we won't allow this to happen.

Third, he responds to the question, What does it mean to be free? He writes:

> . . . it is not necessary that I should be indifferent as to the choice of one or the other of two contraries; the contraiwise the more I lean to the one—whether I recognize clearly that the reasons of the good and the true are to be found in it, or whether God so disposes my inward thought—the more fully do I choose and embrace it.

It is significant to remind ourself of a basic premise here, namely, the knowledge of the understanding should always precede the determination of the will. He has something more to say about this, because he insists that the will always retains the power of directing itself towards one side or the other apart from any determination by the understanding.

Is this a good example of a paradoxical position? Not at all. The human will is always undetermined from without—though it is not always indifferent to the alternatives confronting it. The agent gets into a cognitive and conative bind when the agent does not know what is the more true or the better, or at least when he does not see clearly enough to prevent him from doubting about it. Thus the indifference which attaches to human liberty is very different from that which belongs to the divine.

What is he saying? The divine is a given? Is the only freedom man possesses in a universe in which both man and the divine are cooperatively active? Are the ends of which he speaks realized only in First Cause as Absolute? Can such a concept of freedom exist without the moral demand being met which is inherent in the concept of freedom?

Or, perhaps the question should be phrased, What affect will this have on freedom if there is ". . . recuperation between divine determination, which at the same time produces the differences of the tendencies of will and penetrates them in their attitude by omniscience . . . and responsible human self-activity." The word to note here is responsible.

But, does any of this really necessitate a change in our position? Of course not. He does, however, make us more conscious of some additional thought areas which we must pursue.

What is the True Value of Freedom?

To raise the question about the value of freedom is to instigate another train of thought. For instance, is freedom what man really wants? What about the security factor attached to an authority figure which assumes all responsibility for the agent and his actions? If the agent moves on the assumption that all decisions have already been made for him, the question of freedom does not arise nor, is he particularly bothered about being held responsible for what is done. Inherent in this position is a second question, is it even possible to suggest that freedom then is to be listed among the greatest *goods* open to man?

For the mind willing to delegate its authority and responsibility, the above questions are relevant. However, for the self-actualizing mind, one in the process of making meaning for itself because it has become a self-determiner, the questions are irrelevant.

There are questions which we feel are relevant to our position. These include: (1) Wherein lies the source of value in freedom? (2) What are the epistemological premises upon which the mind must base its methods if it is to realize the potentiality inherent in value for freedom? (3) Because the mind is free to choose (even free to choose to relinquish its freedom to authority), does this factor alone suggest that the value of freedom is conditional, that is, contingent upon decisions made by the mind? (4) Or, are we suggesting that because freedom itself is not conditional, but only the value attached to it, freedom is a given, therefore, an absolute? (5) Does this not suggest that herein lies the true value of freedom?

This would mean that all other value is secondary in nature, and not to be confused with the absolute quality of freedom itself.

In response to some of the questions raised above we raise a number of others. (1) Is it possible to consider choice as an existent if the mind is not absolutely free to make a choice? (2) Will the free mind even make a choice unless it is able to assure itself (the method is important here) that the choice carries the label of an absolute good? (3) Is it possible for the mind to function freely if there is some question (raised by itself) about the particular nature of freedom rather than possessing an absolute nature?

The real question we raise then, is about the true value of freedom. Is it to imply that "freedom (or rather ability) had acquired a value of its own"? Hardly. Before it is able to do this, as a part of the cognitive and conative process of the mind, it has to possess a value, namely, the absolute quality of its giveness; it is from this premise that freedom develops the secondary qualities or values known as mind potentialities.

CHAPTER FOUR

CHOICE

To consider the problem of choice in its relation to will is to ask the question, Must I will before I make a choice; must I make a choice in order to act? When I act, does this imply physical movement; are we willing to concede to the suggestion that what we are speaking of is a mental act as well as a physical movement? Now, these are legitimate questions and certainly have a place in our thinking at this point in the discussion; but, together, they confront us with another question, namely, When I choose, is my choice one of action? What we are really asking is, Is choice itself an action? If I have made a choice, the mind has moved; is this movement the action, or is it the choice I have made? Moreover, I would not have made the choice if I had not willed it; is it the will which has moved? Can we separate will from mind? Can we separate mind from its actions which result in a choice? Is choice a passive resultant of the action of the mind?

For just a moment, let us shift our epistemological gears and approach our problem from a different angle. We move from this assumption: the self-determined mind has willed to choose; the choice has been made and now I am free to act. The question now arises, Since I am free to act, and I do act, does this imply that the act thereby, because it is free action, is always chosen? This question may present some difficulty; let me explain it more fully. When I started writing this morning, I removed my suit coat and placed it on a nearby chair. After an hour of writing, I felt a bit chilled. Here is a value condition. I make a value judgment: I was cold, so I willed to make a choice, to remove the coat from the chair and place it over my shoulders; or, to remain chilled, with the chance of catching a cold, but also knowing that I write more easily if I am not too comfortable. I could not make a choice until I had taken into consideration these conditions, and I could not act until I had made a choice. Now, we come to the question under consideration. I move as a self-determined mind; I am free to act. If I wish, I can leave the coat where it is. However, after evaluating all the conditions, I act and put the coat on my shoulders. The act was free action; was it chosen? I choose to put my coat on my shoulders; in this case, without question, it was a chosen act.

The scene changes. The setting is the same. All the conditions are identical. I have willed my choice; this time, not to act. The coat is to remain on the chair, and I will take the chance of catching a cold. My reason: If I am a bit uncomfortable, my writing will progress more rapidly. While I am deep in thought and writing, and my left hand is partially covering my eyes, my wife comes very quietly into the room, lifts the coat from the chair, and before I realize it, the coat is on my shoulders, against my will, and not of my choice.

The analogy is a strained one. Here was an act, there was movement, something happened to me which was against my will; the action was free, but it was not mine. It was not chosen by me.

It must be remembered that actions, while they may occur in concert, are extremely personal in nature. If I make a choice together with someone else, I am still making the choice as an individual. It is the individual who must be free to act, and when he does act, what he has done has been done freely, and the free action then has been chosen. On the other hand, if this freedom does not exist, we have an entirely different problem facing us. If the action is not free, the choice likewise cannot be free.

Is it possible to make a choice in which the free action does not exist?

We return to the case of the coat. I made my choice, the coat is to remain on the chair. Here is free action. The coat remains on the chair because I so willed it. Now, is it possible for me to make a choice such as: I am cold, so I am going to put on my coat. I reach over to the chair and try to remove it, but it remains stuck to the chair. Unknown to me, during the moments I was away, someone placed adhesive on the chair and now the coat is securely fastened. These conditions do not change the nature of our problem, however. There was no free action even though I had chosen to put on the coat, but our working premise remains the same. The free action in reference to the choice remains the same; conditions exist which did not permit my removing the coat; a determinant was at work which now refers to the action alone, and not to the choice.

Thus, it is necessary to restate our question. I was free to act, but the object of my choice was not free in the sense that it was possible to remove the coat. When I acted (tried to remove the coat), what I was doing was done freely; this action was done freely and it had been chosen. Freedom did not exist, however, to the degree that I could actually remove the coat; in this case, there was no free action; free action now relates to the intended action rather than to the choice. My choice remains the same; I was free to make it. But I was not free to actualize the choice. All of this, of course, does not disturb the proposition made three paragraphs ago, when it was stated: If the action is not free, the choice likewise cannot be free. This refers to the free action of the choice.

There is another point at which some question may be raised. We must not forget the subtlety implied in any action. My choice was to remove my coat from the chair; what is the real choice? Is the emphasis to be placed on the word remove? Perhaps. The choice is between leaving the coat on the chair, or, removing it, so that I can place it on my shoulders. In order to remove it, I must stand, use my hands and arms, etc. What I am saying here is that the choice, in this instance, is determining the type of activity and action necessary to remove the coat, so that the choice will be realized. Here is an example of the action relating to choice, and what is free, even though the first action relating to the actual lifting of the coat is stopped by a determinant unknown to the mind making the first choice. New conditions have now arisen, requiring new choices.

There is another aside which must be examined. I chose to remove the coat from the chair and place it on my shoulders. In the choice, I knew it would be necessary to stand, extend my arms and hands, and take the coat and put it on my shoulders. There was no other way to actualize my choice (to remove from the chair and place on my shoulders rather than leave the coat on the chair) unless I asked someone to do it for me. This, in itself, would not change the nature of the problem. The question now arises, was it, in the first place, accidental that I made my choice to act? Not at all. The conditions were such that I was cold, and I willed, because I valued health more than speed in writing, to put on the coat. There was nothing accidental about it. However, could there have been something accidental about it? In one sense, yes. When I arrived at my desk, without thinking, I could have removed my coat without taking into consideration the temperature of the room. It was not until I became chilled that I realized my need for the coat. This does not make the second choice accidental. That is, to put on my coat. We can say the first choice was accidental. That, perhaps out of habit, I removed the coat without examining the conditions. Here the mind was not functioning as a self-determined mind. Even here we find it difficult to suggest that what is done and out of habit is accidental. What has been patterned, therefore determined, is hardly accidental. Moreover, could we say that it was only by chance that I did not do otherwise? If we now begin to follow this line of reasoning, the end is already in view, because this is where it will take us. If it is matter of chance, because it was accidental that I took off my coat, doing as I did, because I had not made a choice, or, if I did, it was made for me because of the strength inherent in habit, does such action imply that the mind cannot be held responsible if accident and chance usurp the role of mind in ordering choice?

The lines of the argument are not clear; they have been made fuzzy for the sake of discussion, and hopefully, clarification.

There is an interesting relationship here that must be taken into consideration, namely, between accident and responsibility. The statement "accidents will happen" is often heard. Indeed, they do happen and, at times, they are willed to happen. Or, perhaps we should state it in this way: accidents are permitted to happen; for instance, because of some carelessness. The question of responsibility should not arise if the accident has been willed, or permitted, to happen. The mind is responsible in these instances. If there is a real accident, the conditions were such that I could not help it; it was beyond my control.

For instance, am I responsible for this accident? Each morning I write at the university library. I sit on the same chair at the same desk near the same window. This has been a practice for many years. During this time I have come to trust the chair; never is there any hesitation to sit on it. This morning I again repeated my schedule. However, as I sat on the same chair it collapsed and I was thrown to the floor. An accident happened. Was it my responsibility? For what? Because the chair collapsed? It was my weight which broke it. But, would there not be the suggestion, at least, of a flaw in the design or in the wood itself? This certainly would not be my responsibility. My responsibility because the accident happened? There was no reason to suppose that it would happen. Because of all the tenuous circumstances surrounding the accident, would it not be better to write it off as an accident? And, perhaps blame it on the chair or, on the person who weakened it in the first place? Or, on the wood, or, on the designer? Perhaps such a reaction is justified.

Perhaps we should ask other kinds of questions, all of which may suggest a very extreme position. What if the mind believes that anything is possible? When I go to my office, the ceiling may cave in, or the chair collapse. Is my responsibility to stay out of my office and off my chair? A bit ridiculous. And yet, the possibility is there.

There is responsibility in all this, however. That is, to the point of awareness; in other words, if the ceiling is rapidly cracking and beginning to sag, am I going to sit under it, waiting for it to fall? Again, a bit ridiculous. If my chair sways and creaks, groaning every time I sit on it, and do nothing but sit on it again and again, is this being responsible? I am now aware of the complications of the conditions. Awareness tells us that knowledge is possessed of the condition. Without this knowledge, responsibility does not enter the picture.

On the other hand, if I have the responsibility to know, here again, is a factor which cannot be overlooked. In a pure accident, there is no intention; without intention, there is no responsibility. But the accident willed or permitted is caused by intention, and the causer is responsible. When we ask the question, Could the accident have been avoided? and the answer is yes, because we did not assume the responsibility to do whatever was necessary to avoid it, we respond to the first sentence of this paragraph. The question then, must be asked, Was it an accident? An accident exists (happens) only when human responsibility cannot be attached to it in any way. Accidents come into being when human intention is not present.

There is another interesting relationship here. Is it possible for the mind to make a mistake and the result of the mistake be the accident? Of course. The intellective process makes many mistakes and often its data is incomplete. But again, we must ask, If there is a mistake because of inadequate or incomplete data, is the result an accident? Is what is caused in this way to be excused? Is anything but the true accident excusable? If the data was known, the accident would not have happened. It could have been avoided. A mistake? Yes. An accident? No.

Accidents do happen; but it must be remembered that they have a cause. While it is conceivable that an accident could happen by choice, if it was by choice it was no accident. There is always the grey area surrounding our problem such as I feel, not by choice, but because I was careless. Was I careless by choice? To be careless, must we decide to be careless, or is carelessness a frame of mind, a mental stance? Does not even this require a mind-set which is, in a sense, a choice? Where does all this leave us, epistemologically speaking?

If no choice is involved? There is no question about the relationship between responsibility and the admission that choice was involved. What about choice and chance? I made my choice, and I did so freely. It wasn't by chance that the choice was made, nor was it accidental. The point I wish to make is that, in the first place, we are making a distinction between conditions. The coat is on the chair, for me to remove, if I so will it. Why was it placed on the chair, in the first place? By accident? If so, there was also the chance that I could have left it on, in spite of the fact that I am a creature of habit? If this had been true? Because the moment I removed the coat, without thinking I may have been slightly chilled.

Regardless of how we invent new settings or situations, logical or non-logical, when I decided to remove the coat or put it on, if I consciously made my choice, or habit directed my actions, a choice was made and there is always "some causal explanation" of my choice. This means that choice is always determined; either it is determined by such things as habit, or it is determined by the self-determining mind. Our point in this discussion has been to suggest that before we move on to a clarification of many of the points raised, it is necessary to have clearly in mind, the working assumptions of determinism; it is with respect to choice that our definition of the types of determinism stand best to serve us.

In the above discussion, we have opened the debate concerning the relationship between choice, freedom and causal determinism. We have attempted to do no more than place our epistemological cards on the table suggesting, in their placement, some of the problems which face us when we are forced to consider the cognitive implications of the causal if.

As we now proceed to unfold our argument, two approaches are to be followed. First, using the case study approach, a number of propositions will be proferred; each proposition will be discussed with reference to the coat case. Second, because we believe it will be possible to get at the problems in the relationship between choice, freedom and causal determinism and thereby determine the working relationship between these three constructs, additional questions will be raised, under different headings, suggesting yet different relationships, to encourage us to use the conclusions by applying them to other settings.

Proposition One: choice implies that the mind is free to make a decision; among the alternatives, not only is there the opportunity to choose one from among a number, but each alternative is a definite possibility, the conditions of which make it possible for the mind to actualize its choice.

We return to the coat. When I came into the room and approached my writing table, I was free to make a number of decisions. I could have left the coat on my shoulders, removed it and placed it on the chair, and even after feeling chilled, could have decided not to put it on. Or, I could have chosen to put it on again. The opportunity to choose one was present and, as I learned, each alternative was a definite possibility. No one had placed adhesive on the chair so that I could not remove the coat. Thus, it was possible for the mental action to actualize its choice. However, if the conditions had been such as it would have been impossible to remove the coat, if that had been my choice, new decisions and choices would have been required.

I think it is almost impossible to question the logic inherent in Proposition One. Nevertheless, there are a number of mooted points which should not be ignored. The first has to do with the problem, if there is one, between types of choices. Let me explain. I willed to decide, and therefore I chose to remove my coat and place it on the chair. There was physical action in this instance; to remove the coat it was necessary to lift my arms, etc. Now, if I had made the choice not to remove the coat, the action would have been purely mental, and yet willed. Even though we have discussed this type of action elsewhere, that is, believing, as we do, that all physical action is primarily mental action, this does not speak to our question in its entirety.

Out of this comes one question, Does will express itself only in mental activity such as willing to leave the coat on the shoulders, requiring no physical activity? Because the choice might have been willed to remove it, now requiring physical activity, such activity being delegated to the cognitive and affective domains? Hardly. For when the choice was made, it was made from among a number of alternatives, each of which requiring different types of activity and known to the mind in the process of making its choice. The will is always conscious of the complications and responsibilities of the choices made. This means that the will functioning as the totality of mind was fully aware of the need to lift the arms if one choice was to be made. In other words, there is the awareness, on the part of the will, that what begins as pure mental activity may have to become physical activity. There is a persistent consciousness which is the will which makes it aware of the implications of its processes, the organicity of its relationship to the cognitive and affective constructs. At all times, the will is conscious of the implications of its activity, whether mental, physical, or both, as ultimately, both become one.

There is a second mooted point over which we must spend a moment or two. It is true that there were a number of alternatives; the question now arises, was the choice based on the value-priority inherent in the alternatives? If so, what affect does such choice have upon the will and its action? Or, did I will to choose one alternative because I had already decided that it carried the greatest value for me? If I kept the coat on my shoulders, I would not have been chilled but, I would not have progressed as rapidly in my writing. But this is only one facet of the value judgment. What governs the will in making the value judgment in the first place? What determines the rank in the priorities among the alternatives? The answer is, Whatever holds the greatest value for the mind in its totality. But even this answer begs the question. For the mind is concerned about this: Why does a particular alternative hold the greatest value? The answer to that question is this. It is the depth of potential freedom which gives to value its meaning. Thus, when a choice is made from among alternatives, it is willed because of what the choice can come to mean because of the degree of freedom it can bring to the mind. In other words, with the coat off, and a little uncomfortable, I can write much faster. Is speed then, the essential ingredient in the goal already established? But speed may reduce, in this instance, my freedom to carefully evaluate each word which has been written. On the other hand, with the coat on, speed may be limited, but I have greater freedom to what I have otherwise willed as necessary, that is, the need to taste each written word and determine its quality.

There are alternatives in every choice; otherwise, there could be no choice. Among these alternatives, some offer more value, because of their potential for freedom. Of this, the mind, by means of its intellective process, seeks to know more. Until the mind is satisfied, the will wills not to will; the mind as will, wills when it is assured that the chosen value will guarantee it freedom of action.

Proposition Two: potentiality for freedom lies with the knowledge space of the mind; freedom cannot be used as opportunities unless the mind is conscious of its freedom and knows, as a self-determiner, the conditions of that freedom. Before we discuss the implications of this proposition, let us review one of our positions which affects the proposition itself. If the mind is not a self-determiner, then it is determined by conditions which take from it both authority and responsibility. This implies there is no freedom of choice, nor is there potentiality for freedom. So our proposition relates to the self-determined mind, one free to make choices, and knows the freedom to pursue the opportunities which freedom alone proffers. This means the mind is free to choose one from a number of alternatives. Thus, there is the potentiality for freedom, because this potentiality lies within the knowledge space of the mind. Part A of the proposition is then, in reality, saying opportunities cannot be pursued unless they are known to exist, as well as their potentiality for being known. Ignorance delimits the opportunities of the mind; such a factor controls alternatives, and therefore serves as a determiner of mind. With the freedom to know, opportunities become potentialities; the greater (deeper) the knowledge, new relationships are formed and new perspectives come into being; with new perspectives new horizons suggesting opportunities appear.

Without knowledge, the mind is blind to what consciousness is opening as opportunities for exploration. It is knowledge which, as a result of the intellective process, determines the degree of freedom inherent in the mind's relationship to the learning object, and which determines the degree to which the mind, as subject, can experience the potentiality of its object. The question is, What are the opportunities for knowing the object?; herein lies the degree of freedom already possessed by the mind. This is determined by the depth of knowledge possessed, as well as by the way the mind uses its determined freedom. The above statement cannot be made upon any other assumption than that it is only in freedom that the mind can determine the extent of the freedom it possesses and, in turn, determine the real potentialities in the opportunities which freedom alone brings into focus. Without freedom, consciousness is not aware of its freedom.

1. The Relationship Between Choice and Action

Since we have posited the tenet that choice is an action, mental by nature, is choice to be considered an entity, entirely separate and distinct, from its resultant, the action? Because there is an action, a choice has been made by the free mind; choice is a mind-action, and cannot be separated from its resultant.

> If a philosopher maintains that all actions are produced by ante-cedent choices, an infinite regress arises. For if choices are actions, they must be preceded by choices, which, because they are also actions, must by preceded by still other choices; thus, we are led to the absurdity that no one can act until he performs an infinite number of choices.

There is nothing absurd about believing that choices are mental constructs. They are actions of the mind which act on conditions which must be considered before action can be taken. There is an epistemological logic here which must not be forgotten. My mind acts to choose and when I choose, it is to act. Before there is action, there is choice, and perhaps many of them, but not in terms of "an infinite regress." One of the choices of a free mind is to determine the potentiality of the choice resulting in an action. For me to choose to lift the library building in which I am writing, if I mean by lift to do it myself with my hands, is an absurdity. So I must qualify my statement, putting conditions on the choice. For I know it is possible to lift the building with the proper and adequate heavy moving equipment of the building contractor. Here is possibility inherent in choice.

There is, though, an epistemological subtlety here over which we must not glide. If I believe that I can climb the tree outside my window, in a sense, within that statement of belief I have made at least one choice. Because I believe it can be done, I can choose to climb it, if I will it. In stating my belief, I already considered a number of considerations such as: personal health, agility, position of the lowest branch as well as the possibility of reaching the other branches, the height of the tree, its girth, whether or not it would hold me, etc. Thus, I believe I can climb the tree, and so I will to choose (the mental action), and I will to act upon making the choice: I climb the tree. Only the free mind is in a position to make such a choice. My mind would not be free to make the choice if, for instance, the state of health, or a broken leg, would not make the choice a feasible one. Here is the logic of a mind which knows itself. It is in this logic that we see how and why the free mind holds itself accountable for its actions. This is an important concept to the mind; it is the means whereby the mind continues to function as its own self-correcting agency.

Question number three. We have spoken of conditions. Is the necessity characteristic inherent in every condition? We have to ask the question, Necessary for what? By their nature, conditions are necessary to be known by the mind, if an action is to be actualized. My broken leg is a condition; it is a necessary condition in the sense that the condition tells me to choose not to choose climbing the tree. It is true that I can choose to climb the tree in spite of the broken leg. In another sense, then, each condition confronts the mind with the need for a different kind of choice. Because of the broken leg, and because I am determined to climb the tree, it is now necessary to use a number of ropes and pulleys, which will hoist me from limb to limb. This, of course, would force us to further qualify the meaning of the word climb. The alert mind is careful of the language it uses.

The subtlety is not answered in full. I am sitting in the Botanical Gardens in Oxford. I am reading, my knees are crossed, and I am munching on a piece of candy. In a moment, a small bird lands on my knee, stares at me with a hungry look. My first reaction is to place a piece of candy on the tip of my finger and offer it to the bird. But I did not act; did I choose not to act? Certainly, and for a number of reasons, one of which was, I did not want to be bothered by an overly friendly bird. I had too much work to do. But, if I had chosen to act, and I began to extend my arm and hand, and suddenly there was a severe muscle twinge; the pain became so great that I could not extend the arm further. Does this affect the choice? Of course not. Does it affect the action? Of course. At this point, a new determinant came into the relationship between choice and action, and the action (first prompted by choice) was not completed. Here was an action which was not decided by the mind, one not completed because the conditions were changed in the process of actualization, and to which the mind quickly adjusted. In this way, it corrected its choice; if the mind had known of the possibility of the muscle spasm, because there had been warning signs, no doubt the first choice would have been not to offer the bird a piece of candy.

2. The Problem of Honesty in Choosing

How honest am I when I make a choice? Is honesty a problem here? This morning I decided to wear a tweed coat with a sprinkling of orange and brown in the fabric. It is a favorite coat. With that particular coat I prefer to wear a gold shirt, but I know my daughter has repeatedly said: With that coat, wear the orange shirt, because . . ." Now, I have a strong dislike for the orange shirt, but I chose it, nevertheless.

Was I being dishonest? Hardly. I simply made a choice, on the basis of the reasons which held the greatest value for me. That is, I accepted my daughter's recommendation; this became my choice, and I wore the orange shirt.

Let us look at the problem from a different point of view. My choice is the gold shirt; moreover, I have my reasons for making this choice. Is it possible that my choice is false? Not if it is within the realm of possibility for me to wear the shirt, and the given reasons stand as validated. This is quite different from attempting to climb a tree with a broken leg. Would it make any difference to the nature of our problem if I had made the choice before considering the suggestion made by my daughter? No, because it was still my choice; but now, for new reasons, which are acceptable, a new choice is in order. Even though, in the resources of my mind, I still prefer the gold to the orange shirt, the choice itself and the reasons attached thereto, remain. Moreover, even if I were to say to her, I prefer the gold, thereby asserting my real choice, if I wear the orange, I still do so because of a choice. Again, the nature of the problem is not changed. Here my first choice is the gold shirt, but I wear the orange one. This is the second choice, and it has superceded the first, doing so because of value priority.

3. The Question of Decision and Its Relation to Choice

My first choice was not my decision. My decision was to wear the orange shirt. The decision reflected the second choice; nevertheless, it was a choice, with all the reasons attached thereto. In actuality, my mind had delimited the choices; I had two choices, my choice, the gold one; the other, that of my daughter, the orange one. The choice was to be between them. It is also important to remember that I had decided to choose; it was to be one or the other. Because I had decided to choose, here was will, and by the will, I would make a choice. The scene may change. Because I now decided to please my daughter, I chose the orange shirt. In reaching for it, however, I noticed that the cuff was cut. The conditions are now changed. It is no longer possible to wear the shirt of my choice, to act in accord with my decision. All of this confronts us with a new question. Is decision implied in choice? "I decide to choose . . ." I have already made a choice, to decide to choose or not. In choice, I decide for the gold or orange shirt. I act, by putting on the orange shirt. When I act, by putting on the orange shirt, my decision has been actualized. Perhaps it is more correct to suggest that choice is implied in decision; decision is implied in choice.

4. The Difficulty in Making a Choice

Perhaps this is why it is often so difficult to make a choice. The thing which complicates our thinking at this point is the idea of intention. I fully intended to wear the gold shirt, but after giving it a great deal of thought (meaning, I considered conditions which up to this time I was unwilling to consider, but now, am willing to allow to enter my consciousness for consideration) new values have surfaced which hold particular meaning for me; my original intention is changed; I now intend to follow the suggestion of my daughter.

Intentions do change; we must be aware of the fact that they will change when they are given sufficient reason for doing so. There is, however, another facet to our question. Our problem becomes more complicated when we add this dimension. While I intended to wear the gold shirt because, for me, it was the best choice, my value judgment changed because of new value conditions. This, in itself, makes for more difficulty in choosing. But what happens to the original intention? Does the intention change? In one sense, no. For without the new or added conditions, the intention remains unmoved. There is the one thing about intention, though, which changes the question. In a second sense, intention does change. *Intention wants me to make the best possible choice.* And so, it was really not the gold shirt which was intended, although this was my choice, but whatever shirt was best matched for the coat. It is intention which constantly suggests the need, not so much to make a choice, as to make the best possible choice, taking all conditions into consideration.

5. How Does the Mind Make the Best Possible Choice?

Intention has alerted me, since I have decided to make a choice, to the need to make the best possible choice. Because I intended to wear the gold shirt, the decision was made for good and acceptable reasons; in other words, I had made up my mind to wear that particular shirt, until . . . When my daughter confronted me with new potentialities for thought, the question of choice was reopened. The mind was open to reconsideration. If I had become stubborn and set my mind against further thought, I would have broken faith with intention, that is, to make the best possible choice. It is conceivable that I could have said, My closet has a number of shirts which might be worn with this coat, and one of which is the orange one. But I have decided not to consider this problem any further. Would the mind be right in taking such a position, since the gold one was deemed the best choice? This question only begs the problem. To close the mind to new opportunities for choice, which may supercede what has, at this point, become perhaps only desire, is to destroy the purposive mind of intention.

Like intention, desire and preference changes. With the choice of the orange shirt, intentions now become identified with the change, since it has now been decided that it is the best possible choice. Moreover, I desire what is best, so the orange shirt becomes my preference for whatever reasons were acceptable in the value conditions.

This does not exclude the idea that my desire bends toward gold shirts, much in preference to orange ones. It is just that in certain conditions new value judgments are demanded because new relationships may require new priorities, for the moment.

Nor, does it exclude the possibility that I could have acted irrationally. However, to be irrational is to have the mind closed by determinants or, the self-determined mind can place closure on itself and refuse to think further on a matter. This position has been discussed above.

The circle of argument is not yet closed. Another question faces us. How do I know that when the mind has made the best possible choice, it is the best choice, since only mental action has taken place, and the choice itself has not been actualized? It is December, and I am in the process of making a decision. There are two main alternatives from which to choose. My concern is with next summer. The question is whether or not to spend part of the summer in Europe or, to spend the same period at our lake home. After appraising all the conditions, I have chosen not to return to Europe for at least two years; so, the time is to be spent at our lake home. To actualize this choice means many months are to elapse. How, then, do I know this was the best choice? It is conceivable that after spending some weeks at the lake, I might conclude: how much better it would be spending this time in some of my favorite European haunts.

Yes, this may happen. And, it will happen if new priorities for consideration are brought forth. There are two things we may wish to remember in this connection. First, whatever choice is made, is contingent upon the conditions and circumstances of the moment. As of nine a.m., I have decided not to eat lunch. But, at eleven forty-five a.m., the conditions may be such that I will change my mind; the best choice, because of new conditions, now supercedes the first best choice. Second, there may be a considerable time lapse between choice and final action. Unless new conditions arise, which now suggest a reappraisal of conditions, the first best choice stands. The thing to remember here is that the self-determined mind functions, by means of its intellective processes, as a self-corrector. It it finds that a decision is not the best one after all, it does not hesitate to make whatever changes are deemed more valuable.

6. Is There an Ethical Base for this Concept of the Mind as a Self-Corrector?

It should be evident in the foregoing discussion on choice that it is our belief that, in choice, we have the pivotal concept in ethics. While this concept is discussed in greater detail elsewhere in the book, the question is in order and in place. One of our basic assumptions with respect to action is the contention that we do what we believe; in other words, morality is reflected in action itself. There is one qualification to this proposition, namely, this is both the mental action which is choice, and the actualization of the choice, the doing of the choice. The ethical base rests upon this assumption. To divide the actions is to raise additional problems in the ethical stance. This is to be seen in the ethical bind which may arise in a mind which easily contradicts itself. If I say that I will do what I believe, I may find myself in this predicament. The key here is the knowledge factor. I believe that I am able to climb the tree outside my window, that is, if the conditions are such as to make it possible. For, if the conditions make it possible, then I will do it. Only when I know, without question, that something can be done, will I do it. Now, I may try to climb the tree without knowing the conditions; such a position is affected by another dimension of ethicism. The ethical base is the epistemological realization of the possible. I believe because, taking all conditions and circumstances into consideration, it is possible to climb the tree, unless . . . there are conditions about which I could know nothing, and this does not affect my ethical choice.

I have a reason(s) why I believe, and why I do, what I do; upon the premise of belief, I act; sometimes it may be on the basis of incomplete knowledge, knowing that complete knowledge is not available. I make my choice upon what knowledge I possess, deeming it sufficient, though incomplete, to assure me that what I am doing is the right thing.

It is only the self-determined mind which is willing to accept responsibility for its actions; and, of course, responsibility accepted as such, is the working hypothesis from which the intellective process moves.

When it was stated that I have a reason(s) why I believe, the mind is saying to itself: It is necessary to know why there is that particular belief. This is the same as saying: If I am responsible, and I accept the fact that I am, what is there in the why which allows me, in the first place, to accept the responsibility, as well as to determine the working base from which the principles, allowing the action, have evolved. The decision is always a personal one in the same way the relationship between mind and belief is personal. One part of this process suggests the need for self-validation. This means nothing more than knowing (by degrees of apprehension) and valuing the reasons for belief and, on the basis of this relationship, there is the willingness to act.

The philosopher Kant raises an interesting point in this connection. The reason we listen to him at this point in our discussion is because of a forced relationship; by this is meant: our position holds no alternative to the belief that the process of knowing is a personal one, which the mind does because the mind is its intellective process; what governs is, in this instance, what we define as the cognitive, affective and conative domains. The mind is all three domains. When Kant speaks of the autonomy of the will, suggesting this as a condition (which is somewhat confusing), we ask, A condition of what? If it is the condition suggesting the dependency upon the cognitive and the affective, the strength of the relationship resting upon the degree of interaction necessary for any one of them to function, our problem has been clarified. We speak often, in this study, of the moral agent, and now we attach a will to the agent. The question now arises, is this will, of the moral agent, a law to itself? Or, to ask it more succinctly, is there a condition in which the will ever acts autonomously? Is Kant's proposition, that an analysis of the concepts of morality would show us that the principle of autonomy is the sole principle of ethics, a valid one? Our answer, only if the will is conceived as a function, in which the cognitive and the affective domains have been used, and the will is being emphasized as a function of the total mind. It does, however, assist us to recognize the legitimacy of considering belief and its relational base to action as a moral question which the mind knows it cannot ignore.

7. Since There is This Ethical Base, as an Epistemological Existent, Does It Destroy the Concept of Freedom in its Relation to Choice?

To answer this question, we shall first take another look at our above discussion pertaining to Kant's autonomy. We evidenced a bit of epistemological concern, and so the question of condition was raised in reference to Kant's position of making the will completely spontaneous and free. Our reaction is one of further question: Can such a concept of will be completely free and spontaneous and then be labelled pure as Kant conceives of will? If you recall, the question of condition was injected because of a basic dependency factor suggesting that will, as one functional domain of mind, in order to function, is dependent upon the cognitive and affective domains as well. What does this have to say about freedom and choice?

This can best be answered by considering a position quite different from Kant's. I refer to St. Thomas. If these two men had lived at the same time, no doubt the debates between the two would have been vigorous. St. Thomas would have been quite skeptical about many of Kant's propositions, especially about the spontaneity idea, and certainly about the way we somehow must interpret his position on the autonomy of the mind. Aquinas finds such a stand impossible to accept. He cannot attribute either spontaneity or autonomy to the will. His reason for this attitude is both clear and concise: the self-determining act of the will is free choice. Upon this premise his entire position on epistemology rests. The premise, of course, is based on a number of assumptions, the first of which is not always clear and concise. Perhaps it is only a problem in semantics. The assumption is this, and it is in this first statement we find our problem. He speaks of the will as willing or not willing. And yet, the mind of his writings seems to suggest that the will always wills, and it is not a question of whether or not to will. In other words, if the decision is not to will, it is always free to do so. There is a power of the will; what is this power and what is its source? Within that power lies the freedom not to will and therefore not to act. Perhaps there is no problem.

The question of free choice is pivotal in Aquinas' thought. This is true because of what he conceives of as the depth of the relationship between will and reason (reasons) in cause. While this is discussed in detail elsewhere, it is sufficient here to remind ourselves that there was no wavering on Aquinas' position that the act of choice (the self-determining act)—only because the mind is self-determining—as will, can be free or caused. It isn't necessary for his use of 'caused' to throw us into an epistemological dither. He is a very consistent thinker. Causation, for Aquinas, is a special kind of concept, one which very carefully must be defined, particularly from the emphasis upon the potentiality causations for free choice. He tells us that it is the will which determines that the cognitive domain apprehends, from First Cause, its reasons, not only for existence, but in what has been caused, and the potential meaning, when realized, for the mind. It is then up to the totality of the mind to judge what the nature of the relationship is to be between itself, what the choice (if it is made) portends, and the need to act, considering both the time factor and adequate methodology for complete apprehension.

We said above that Aquinas acquaints us with the power of the will. The above proposition can be achieved only because the will possesses this power. Its source, without question, is a spirituality of the total mind, a placement which tells us that the will, and its partners cognition and the domain of the affective, originate from an epistemological authority higher than the pure sensate experience of the ill-defined empiricism which Aquinas thinks as totally inadequate. His definition of empiricism grants to empiricism a more substantial essence.

In addition to this, it must be recalled that it is this ethical base that gives to man his dignity. Man does not possess dignity if he is not free to make choices, and do so as a self-determining mind; the will is free only in the self-determined mind. It is only in this context that the consequences of ethics can even be considered. Kant and Aquinas confront us with many of the intricacies of the problem.

CHAPTER FIVE

DETERMINISM

The verb determine is seen as being elusive in literature on epistemology; even the steady hand of the most conservative epistemologist must struggle to maintain its grasp on this slippery concept. While determinism wears its battle scars well, its place in the front lines of the free-will controversy has never been taken by a would-be usurper. Perhaps the deep lines tracing each scar is suggestive of the epistemological pain endured, and sufficient to ward off the faint-hearted. Is there a concept in philosophy, theology, psychology and epistemology more harassed than determinism?

So there will be no question about our usage; these opening paragraphs will define and postulate our assumptions. Since it is an impossibility to even consider the epistemological constructs which make up the concept of determinism without seeing it in its relationship to two other concepts, namely, will and freedom, there are three assumptions which open for us the nature of determinism. These are: (1) there are determinants over which the mind has no control; (2) there are determinants which, because of their nature, can be controlled by the mind; and (3) there is that determinant which can be brought into being which will affect the mind's relationship to the first controllable determinant, thereby changing the nature of the control and its affect upon the self.

An illustration of each assumption is in order.

1. There are determinants over which the mind has no control. It is a beautiful day; there is not a cloud in the sky. A soft breeze is blowing; all the signs are there for a day of perfect sailing. I make my preparations, and raise the sail. For hours, my sailing anticipations were fulfilled; suddenly the wind changes; the intensity of the gusts makes it impossible to continue; I must lower the sail or capsize.

The change of conditions forces upon me certain and very definite alternatives. Even though there is a determinant over which I have no control, alternatives exist. I still have a choice. If I so decide, in spite of the strength of the wind, I can leave the mast and sail in position; but now, another decision confronts me: Do I want to take a chance of capsizing and perhaps drowning? An analysis of conditions tells me how illogical such a stance would be. The presence of cause and its implications and signification is evident. In a sense, this example illustrated only a happening, over which my mind has no control. I had no power over the wind and what it might do to my boat. But, this is not correct. I had no power over the wind and what it would do to my boat, unless I willed to control the affect of the wind upon the boat. All the empirical data was present: unless I lowered the sail, the boat would capsize. So, what we have here are two determinants: the first, over which I had no control whatsoever; the second, over which I had control if I so willed it.

Another example. I am standing before a set of lifting weights. I am determined to lift them. I reach over, brace myself, take hold of them, and lift. But, to no avail. I, then, kneel on the floor, read the size of the weights and realize that I attempted to lift five hundred pounds. Nevertheless, I had been determined to lift them. Here, indeed, was something over which I had no control; here were determinants that no physical and mental preparation could enable me to overcome. Now we come to an important relationship between mind and the so-called determinant over which we have no control. I call it the nature of an on-going responsibility. Wasn't it a bit foolish of me to attempt lifting the weights before I knew how much they weighed? To look at them suggested a mere fifty to one hundred pounds. If I had taken the responsibility of collecting data (finding out how much they weighed) I would not even have attempted to lift them. Isn't there a different kind of choice involved when the mind accepts the responsibility of analyzing the implications of a determinant? It is true there are determinants over which I have no control, but nevertheless, every determinant has built into it the implications of its actions upon the object, such as upon the mind of the self being confronted by the determinant. While I had no control over the determining wind, I did have control, because of what my mind decided to do, over what could happen to the boat. This is a factor which surfaces, however, only when I accept the responsibility of analyzing the implications of the determinant, and the application of these implications upon my particular situation. I did lower the sail, and shifted ballast, and thereby remained upright. If I would not have responded to the empirical and logical eye of responsibility, I would have capsized.

2. There are determinants which, because of their nature, can be controlled by the mind. What is the difference between this assumption and what has been suggested above? To answer this question, we must make a number of distinctions among relationships.

A friend recently suffered a heart attack. This happened in spite of the fact that he had periodic physical examinations, sufficient rest and exercise, diet, etc. The heart attack was a determinant over which his mind had no control; after the attack, his mind concerned itself with the implications of the attack. At this point, his will was fully functional.

The will can be fully functional if the determinant can be controlled by the mind. In one sense, every confrontation serves as a determinant. The responsibility of the mind is to determine its relationship to the determinant. For example, such a passive thing as the tree I pass on my morning walk, quite literally, confronts me; I must decide my relationship to it. On most mornings I totally ignore it, and am not aware of it. On other occasions, I am conscious of a low hanging branch which may force me to walk around it. If I choose not to walk around it, my head will strike the branch. I have determined (controlled) the nature of the relationship. The same setting may confront me with the need to be on the alert in crossing the street, cautious of an unfriendly dog. In all of these instances, the mind was actively engaged in meeting the implications of an act, event or happening which, as yet, remained as a potential in its implications. Now, the point is this. If I wish, I can ignore the implications of the determinant. In spite of the fact that I know the branch is there, the dog is waiting around the corner of the house, or the street, at this time of the day, is always the scene of heavy traffic, I can proceed as though I were ignorant of the implications of these determinants.

To stop at this point in our analysis would indicate, however, an inadequacy in our epistemological perspective.

If I know, for example, that the branch is there, and I ignore the fact that I do know, even here, the will is functional. By the fact that I decide to ignore what I know, is still an act of the will. Moreover, there was some reason, which evidently carried its own logic, for the will to act as it did. The question we then raise is, Did the will cognize the nature of the relationship responsibly? It is conceivable that the eye, seeing the branch, and the mind reacting to its close proximity, decided to take a chance; if my hat was knocked askew, so what? No damage done.

Does the will always function to assure a result which can be classified as good? If there is a rivalry between my neighbor and myself and this morning he brought home a new car, and this upset me, so I decided to play the game of one-up-man-ship, and I bought a model one size larger than his, even though I could ill afford it, nor did I need a new car, what can we say about the reasonableness of the will? This question brings us to the third of our assumptions.

3. There is a determinant which can be brought into being which will affect the mind's relationship to the first controllable determinant, thereby changing the nature of the control and its affect upon the self.

It must be remembered that the will does not function as an entity; it is totally dependent upon the affective and cognitive constructs of the intellective process in order to move. This means that all the dimensions of feeling and the cognitive abilities of the mind combine to feed the will so, together, a decision can be made. This means the will functions from within the totality of mind, and, as mind. It does not make choices and act oblivious to the input of the affective and cognitive domains. The only way in which it can function is by its use of these two domains. Thus, there is a knowledge base for its operations, as well as the limited offerings of sense experience. Because of its need to depend upon these domains, what it now has to work with is a new epistemological tool, namely, perceptive power. It is this power the will brings to every confrontation, and the need arises to determine the nature of the relationship to the confrontation, and become aware of the implications arising from within the relationship. Only then can the will decide upon the nature of its responsibility for acting.

When we say the mind determines its relationship and responsibility to a determinant, this, in itself, is a determinant; with the human mind, there is, with responsibility, the reason which activates movement; this is will. This is a human reaction. Even the inanimate, as a determinant, can force itself, as cause, upon the human self. My mind tells me not to push my automobile. The car may say to me by means of my powers of observation: But I am only a very small car, and not too heavy. Try me, I am stuck in the snow.

What affects the mind's relationship to such a determinant? The answer is a simple one if we are willing to believe that the mind itself is always a determinant, one which can be trusted if it listens to itself and the knowledge it possesses. Even if the car is small, I am not strong enough to push it. When will takes over, because it is acting responsibly, according to reason, the nature of control is changed, the car, as a determinant is not controlling the human mind, the totality of the self as mind, has been affected.

The will, acting responsibly, controls the determinant and its implication upon the human self; but it must not be forgotten that in its control, the self has been affected primarily because the knowledge which it has made available to itself, has been used, by the self, in order to reason. The will acts responsibly when it finds its reasoning potential in the meaningfulness of cause.

1. Reason

It is a logical and valid conclusion when we say, If a determinant exists, whatever it might be, there is a reason for its existence. We noted above that, in one sense, every existent is a determinant because of the possibility of an affect it may have upon me. It may be a stone lying on the street or an abstract thought which persisted in nudging me on the way to the library this morning. Whenever the person of the self enters into any kind of a relationship with an existent, that existent may confront it as a determinant making it necessary for the mind to determine the nature of the new relationship. We have two factors here which must be given consideration. First, there is the assumption that what exists, exists for a purpose which is a part of a larger reason for being. What is, has been caused; when the *is* enters a new relationship now as a determinant and confronts mind, we find the second assumption ready for consideration, namely, there is a reason why the existent has become a determinant. This reason includes such dimensions as: the way in which it has become a determinant, and its potential implications upon the mind of the self as the mind responds by means of its relationship to the determinant.

That stone on the street. I saw it there yesterday. Because I saw it, as an existent, it confronted me with its own being; that is, with what it was. My response was nothing more than, it is a stone lying on the street. This morning, when crossing the street, I did not see the stone and stepped on its edge, turning my ankle. It now served as a new and different determinant, and my relationship to it is quite different. The reason for the new relationship has changed, and my mind is now in relation to the implications of the confrontation and, with sufficient reason, the implications of the fall set up both a new determinant and hypotheses for response and control. There is reason here; reason why I stepped on the stone, reason why I fell, both of which are self-evident. Inherent in reason is cause.

What is the story of will in this? Will responds to confrontation. Together with the other components of the intellective process, it decides what to do now that something has happened. In this case, a high degree of control over the determinant was present. If I had been aware of what was on my walking path, I could have bypassed the stone. However, I did not remember it or see it; as a result, the accident happened. With a high degree of awareness, I would have surveyed the path; if there had been darkness, then I could not have seen it, and would not have been aware of it, if I hadn't seen it yesterday. Nevertheless, all of this is now a matter of historicity; I have fallen, for a reason, and now, for a different reason, I must will my next action. A car is coming and perhaps he does not see me lying in the street. The car is a new determinant; the implications of what the car could do, wills my decisions (I will to do, and do it) and I force my way to the edge of the street, out of danger. In moments, the mind moved based on reasonable data screened by all domains of the intellective process. What I accepted as reasonable data caused me to move very quickly. Now the freedom which the will possesses could have created a passive attitude, and I could have said, The pedestrian has the right of way on this street, and not move. This, of course, suggests that the mind is not acting responsibly. It was possible to move, the danger was there; to will not to move was a refusal to listen to reason. We must be careful to clearly delineate the reasons why the mind wills (or, wills not to will). Perhaps the enclosure is a paradox.

There is an argument which must be looked at a little more carefully. Does decision rest upon the strength of one's reasons for doing what is being done? What validates the reason for a particular action? As I was lying on the street with the injured ankle, knowing that it was possible to move, but saw the car coming and decided not to move because if the car would strike me, I would then be in a position to bring suit against the driver for extensive injuries. Now, it is possible to strongly believe that such action would be to my advantage. My mind (the intellective process) told me differently, however. To will to remain on the street was possible but an action contrary to the real strength in reason.

Is choice ever made without a reason? Would this imply that every choice is then determined? If we choose at random, does this imply the absence of reason? The answer to all these questions is the same. If the determinant is one over which the mind has no control, our problem is an altogether different one. Even then, the mind then moves to consider the implications of the uncontrolled determinant. A determinant beyond the control of the mind does not make it possible for the mind to choose. With the freedom to choose, the mind is then in a position to reason or, for a reason decides not to be reasonable. When the mind is free to choose, the will to act will be based on reason, even though the reason may be in contradistinction to what the perceptive eye of cognition is saying. What is it, then, which validates reason in cause?

2. Cause

To validate reason in cause is a subject discussed in detail elsewhere in the book. However, there are dimensions of the problem which must be studied in a context suggestive of a new emphasis, namely, causal determinism. The reason we make this distinction is because of certain implications made in our discussion of the subject of reason above; implied in every proposition was the question of the relationship between cause and caused, for, implied in this relationship is another new context, the need to understand the working hypotheses inherent in the dependening relationship between determined and caused.

Epistemologists are fond of quoting Bertrand Russell's statement "on the motion of cause" in his *Our Knowledge of the External World* pertaining to the law of universal causation. It is a practical starting point for our discussion of causal determinism.

There are, he says, such invariable relations between different events at the same or different times that, given the state of the whole universe throughout any finite time, however short, every previous and subsequent event can theoretically be determined as a function of the given events during that time.

Here is a good example of "causal deterministic" thinking. On first reading it may cause a degree of consternation, but it need not upset our epistemological premises. Essentially what Russell is saying is that the human being is subject to laws and events over which he has no control. This is true. I have no control over the extremely low temperature registered this morning. Moreover, it determined that if I were not to freeze, it would be necessary to wear heavier clothing than was worn yesterday morning. Essentially, I was free to wear a summer weight suit if I so decided, but then, I would have to pay the consequences. The implications of the very cold weather caused me to reason and will to protect my body. The conditions of the cold were beyond my control, but not the implications of those conditions. In other words, because of what the cold implied; here is a knowledge worked on by the mind. When I recognize the implications of a confrontation, I am aware of the affects of those implications upon me as a total person. This knowing process is the work of the intellective process, one which does not stop with the intellectualizing, but moves toward a decision, the 'what' of being caused. The will moves on what it knows and what the self can become when the choice is made and actualized. This means that there is a consciousness that there are complications, and implications confront the mind with choice. Without consciousness, our problem is a different one, and our interpretation of Russell's words would begin from another premise.

There are other problems here which cannot be ignored, such as, when we speak of laws and events over which the human being has no control, are we speaking of absolutes? One of our epistemological premises is that there are First Principles and First Cause. Now these cannot be spoken of in terms other than the Absolute. Our real problem surfaces, however, when we commit the epistemological sin of equating a causal pre-determinism with the absence of alternatives and then suggest these factors as characteristic of First Cause. To say that the universal laws make it impossible to alter the future is to take away from First Cause its prime intention and purpose. Moreover, such a position would deny the existence of mind among the created human, let alone, the possession of a freedom to make a choice among alternatives. Universal laws do not imply a force, subject to events which cause the mind to react without knowledge or feeling. A tornado is a catastrophic event which *is* for a number of reasons; it has been caused. If I find myself affected by it (conscious of my relationship to it) my mind is free to choose among alternatives, (generated by what has been caused) and cause myself to choose a future not inherent in the power of an impersonal force.

First Cause possesses reasons for what happens. What happens in the physical world of the inanimate and impersonal is purely mechanistic. Mountains remain where they are unless erosion or man changes their profile or removes them completely. The laws governing erosion are still impersonal; there are no causal pre-deterministic laws evolving from First Cause which say: This is what the future will be for that particular man; that is, if he has a working mind governed by the intellective process.

From First Cause inexorable natural laws evolve. These pertain to, and affect, only the physical universe, and the physical organism of the human being which does not function as mind. If the self of the human being does not accept its role of responsibility as a determiner, it becomes subject to the same natural law which says, if you do not protect yourself against the bitter cold, you will freeze. If the human being does not know the implications of the cold, that is, conscious of the danger, our problem again is a different one.

What we said above may suggest that the inexorable natural laws are quite impersonal, particularly since they refer and apply to what does not possess a mind. In this sense, the reaction may be justified, at least in part. We are hesitant though, to suggest there is a complete impersonality attached to natural laws. We say this for a number of reasons. First, natural law is what it is by design of First Cause. Because of this, there is intention and purpose, as characteristic of even the most minute law. Second, First Cause, as the Totality of Mind, the chief characteristic of its nature being its teleological perspective, knows that what has been brought into being has been created for the sake of the mind of the human being, against which he must react and make choices about those things which affect him as a person. Therefore, in quite a different sense, there are no impersonal forces in the realm of created being; what exists stands as a possible source of very personal confrontation to the human mind. In other words, whatever exists may possess some implications for the human mind as it finds itself confronted by the existent. The human mind may decide to remain passive in the relationship, but even this is a decision. Even here the mind is at work; whatever confronts the mind becomes personal by implication of relationship.

The concept of the freedom of the will is not incompatible with determinism. Even will becomes a determiner. There is a causal order inherent in First Cause, and a causal order becomes in second cause. The will always acts within a causal order; the will is unable to function (there is no need to) if the physical determinants make it impossible for the mind to operate through its consciousness. Only in this instance, is the action of the will unpredictable; in consciousness, the will always acts.

We have said that the freedom of the will is not incompatible with determinism. We now move closer to the truly personal factor which changes the nature of determinism and places it within a different context.

Laws exist which, in one way or another, affect, directly or indirectly, the human mind. This is true for every created existent. These laws are what First Cause intended them to be. They do what First Cause intends them to do. Now, since we know what can happen within these laws, such as tidal waves, tornadoes, etc., what does this tell us about the nature of First Cause? Is it the will of First Cause that entire cities be destroyed, and children be separated from parents? Can we rightfully say that the laws themselves are impersonally conceived and intended, and only the implications of their actions are personal in reference? If this is true, does the intention of First Cause become personal when First Cause makes it necessary for the human mind to react and handle that which is happening to it? If there is an a-morality about First Cause, what does this do to the power of reason(s) in cause itself? If there is purpose and intent in First Cause, it cannot be a-moral in nature. If there is purpose and intent in First Cause, its reason for being tells us that it is controlled by those self-creating and self-correcting values which make it impossible to create anything but that which is good. Moreover, through the reason of purpose and intent, First Cause wills that the human mind, by means of knowledge and wisdom in choice, will likewise will what perhaps is first recognized as only an apparent good, but now is seen as the reason of First Cause. This is the highest good, as realized by Aquinas. Man's freedom is found in his own ability to determine the meaning of reason as determined by First Cause. In this context, the human will is determined by the First Will in its reason for the mind to have what is of supreme good. The First Will is determined that the human will comes to know the good, and then determines to actualize it.

Plato was one who wrestled with this problem and found a plausible solution, one which gives meaning to the statements made in the above paragraph. As in every dialogue, he took a very logical approach, building from specific premises. For instance, the question of what constitutes freedom was a very real one for him. His concept of freedom included a close relationship to, and dependency upon, his idea of determinism. There is no such a thing, he tells us, as considering freedom in isolation from determinism. Nor, is it possible to define determinism without noting its relationship to freedom. His conclusion is one which gives us new insight into our problem; it was his belief that freedom is the determinism of the will by what is good; the concept of the apparent good was not sufficient for Plato.

How did he arrive at this conclusion? Before we answer the question, study the logicality of approach. He concerned himself with two basic ideas: first, the problem of choice; the second, the problem of appearance, or, the word 'seems.' It is this last word which may tempt his reader to conclude that he was concerned with the idea of the apparent good. However, his definitions of 'seems' and 'apparent' are quite different. His first premise is this: When mind makes a choice, knowing that such action is always inevitable, such as, deciding not to choose, whatever is confronting him as an object, will be chosen if it seems good. It made no sense to Plato for the mind to choose that which would not be to its benefit. Now we must define the word seem. It is at this point he introduces the word know. In a sense, it is a substitution for the word seem. We change the sentence structure somewhat. He now says: If I know what is good, there is no reason for me to choose something which is not good. But, in true Socratic form, I now ask: Even if I know what is good (absolutely convinced that it is so) isn't it possible for me to choose the opposite? His answer would be, "certainly." But, he says, you will do it in ignorance or involuntarily. Maybe I am not ready to accept this. What if I will to choose the opposite of the good voluntarily? Or, isn't this possible?

His argument persists. He forces me to think in terms of an example. I may choose to ride in an automobile of a friend, because he has invited me to do so. I was ignorant of the fact that he is a fast and reckless driver. However, if I do know these things about his lack of ability as a driver, knowing that, if I ride with him, it is almost inevitable there will be an accident, because my greatest good (at the moment) is my personal safety, I will not to ride with him. My choice was made, because there is no apparency about the object of my decision. Knowing his reputation as a driver, and if he forced me to ride with him, this, of course, would be a matter of acting involuntarily.

Has this answered my earlier question? Knowing what I do, with certainty, about his reputation as a driver, what if I will to ride with him? Then, the object changes, and I will to go with him in spite of the odds, knowing that it is the only way to reach my destination on time.

Plato speaks of knowledge as virtue. It is only logical then, when I know what is good, I will to move towards it. If I move towards something else? An apparent good? No, a good (which is good) if I am willing to gamble in order to achieve it. Moreover, I know it is a goal, but I also know that to will the questionable route is not affecting my freedom which is the determinate to reach what is good.

Knowledge is an important concept to Plato. To knowingly make a choice, and one is able to make a choice only when there is the freedom to do so, the motive for that choice is the knowledge of what is good. Therefore, the action which is voluntary is determined by such knowledge. This tells us Plato was fully cognizant of the interplay among the affective, cognitive and conative domains of the mind. When the mind wills, a joint decision has been made; the incentive is to assure the mind of its continued freedom. The mind is freed by what alone is good.

To pin-point a motive is to study the structural basis of each assumption used by the mind in the making of its decisions. It suggests epistemological blindness to believe that there exists a value-free assumption. Whatever possesses value then, projects a number of implications which the mind must consider while it is in the process of willing action. For the mind not to know its motives is to suggest a mind which is not totally operational. While it is true that motives are often elusive, the fully operational mind knows the degree of imput it must possess in the actual creation of a motive. The mind is not a recipient of motives; it is their creator. It is only in this capacity that it can maintain role in the affective, cognitive and conative dimensions of its responsibility.

With respect to motives, the mind realizes that it must never allow itself to become passive. To do so would imply that certain externals have created motives and now seek to implant them for use by the mind. Motives belong to the mind alone; it is a careful process which is delineated by the mind for their evolvement. While it is true that often motives can get out of mind like actions can get out of hand, for example, in the process of rationalization, it is the responsibility of the validation process and its analyses, to bring out the self-correcting powers of the mind.

Perhaps more than for any other characteristic function of the mind, motives need validation, simply because there are rationalistic dimensions of the mind which refuse to accept the need for validation; again, such as rationalization.

In the first place, we must remember that motives serve as sources of explanation for a particular action.

When I explain a problem in epistemology to my students, is there a difference between this explanation and the explaining which the mind does to itself? Or, we might ask this question, is it possible to explain to another mind without first explaining to the self? Or, as the mind is explaining to another mind, is it during this process the mind explains to the self?

I have now referred to explanation as a process. This means it is a process which always implies self-explanation. Is it possible to explain to another mind until there is a knowlege base from which to move? The mind is unable to function unless the knowledge base exists. The process of self-explanation essentially is the learning process. The teacher aids the learner in the process of the ultimate in learning theory, namely, to take what is offered by teacher or book and assimilate the material of knowledge. This is the process of explaining to the self by one's own mind. There is no full explanation (i.e., meaning) without the mind experiencing itself as explanation.

Learning begins when the mind wills to explain a problem. There is no learning without the mind knowing what is necessary in order to explain what, at one time, was unknown (and may yet be unknown to the mind reviewing the explanation).

Here is our problem. Yesterday after a tutorial based on the philosophical thought of T. S. Eliot, the student asked if I would bring my copy of *Waste Land* to our class today. I replied that I would be happy to do so. Returning home I immediately went into the study, removed the book from the shelf, and placed it on the writing table near my brief case as a reminder to bring it to class. Now the problem is, I did not see the book on the table, and my practice is daily to take my books from that particular spot, and place them in my briefcase. This morning, for some reason this procedure was not followed. As a result, I came to the University without the book which I had promised to bring.

The question, Why? How am I to explain this to the student? What is my reason? It would be very simple to say, I forgot. This explanation usually covers a multitude of epistemological sins. Perhaps such an explanation is justified. But did I forget? What are the reasons for forgetting, if this is what I did? And so I must explain to myself, using the empirical data at my disposal, that is, what the mind knows about the problem.

What does the mind know about the problem? The reason I give to the student may, in part, be correct, such as, I forgot. But, is it the cause for my forgetting? I now proceed to unweave the many strands which, when once again are woven together, will constitute an explanation for my actions, as well as provide me with a meaningful learning experience.

I can say, quite truthfully, I forgot. But why did I forget? What is the cause for the mind stance which allowed me to forget?

When the student asked to see my copy of the *Waste Land* I agreed. I now recall a slight hesitancy, but nevertheless there was agreement. The reason for the hesitancy? It is a causal thing. My copy of the *Waste Land* is an edition long out of print. It would be almost impossible to replace. Moreover, it has been put to much use over a period of many years; its binding is becoming fragile. In addition to this, a number of books loaned to students have never been returned. But, my argument continues, this is a student I know will return the book. So, why the hesitancy? Is it because even though I know the book will be returned, its fragile condition does not suggest that it be loaned? But this I knew before I agreed to bring the book. Have I had second thoughts about an earlier reaction? Yes, we might say that. Or, maybe some of these other factors have been brought into sharper focus. Why, then, did I remove the book from the shelf, place it where I should see it, and then, not see it? Did I know all along that I would not bring the book? Is this why (reasons) I invited the student to our home this evening for dinner and then a period of browsing in my study so that he could see and handle the book without removing it from the room? The cause? In other words, why did I do what I did? The process is clear. I didn't see the book this morning because my will had validated the need to keep the book in my study, even though I had gone through the motions of putting it where I should see it. Such action was willed because the mind had explained to itself, and validated the need to keep the book in the study. The cause now becomes self-evident.

Empirically there was sufficient cause to keep the book in the study; I had maintained a scientific attitude toward the problem. However, the validation process is not without its moral overtones. At times, Kant would have us believe, there is a conflict between moral and scientific interests. Is this possible if we find it necessary to explain cause in light of its teleological nature? And, we do.

As we have acknowledged at every step of our argument, and in every context, there is a determinism which penetrates every dimension of the created order, as well as every facet of the human mind. There is the determinism of an impersonal nature such as the high winds upon the sea, threatening ships and life. These winds are caused and they determine what will happen under certain and specific conditions. Here the human mind is concerned with the personal implications of the impersonal thrusts of a particular force. The mind now must determine the nature of its relationship to these implications. There is the determinism of a personal nature implied in the design and purpose of a created order, ordered by First Cause, with purpose and meaning implied in its nature. The human mind now must determine the nature of its relationship to a Personal Force interested in its ability to function as mind. There is the determinism implied in the human mind in relation to itself, with a need to determine whether or not to allow itself to be determined or, to become a self-determiner. The morality of the problem lies within the nature of the First Cause in its relation to the human mind, as well as in the human mind's knowledge which it possesses within itself, the knowledge which confronts the mind with the realization that it must decide one way or another; that is, to be determined or to be a determiner.

The moral base upon which cause is based is simply this. Regardless of the kind of determinism which confronts the human mind, there are always alternatives present. Even aboard ship, in high winds, with the danger of sinking, I have many alternatives. This is true even though I have no power or control over forces which are determining only generalities. The specifics I take care of for myself, because of the implications which are involved. The question of morality is always implied when choice is present, and since there isn't a determinism working that does not create implications, and my relationship to implications offers me alternatives under any deterministic conditions, I am able to be a self-determiner, if I so determine it. Here is the true nature of the teleological principle at work in determinism. Why I see what I do in every confrontation is the perceiving eye of teleology.

In First Cause, there is Primary Reason inherent in every existent. This means there is reason why the existent is, as well as reason why the existent can become meaningful to the human mind. The premises upon which the mind functions in order to know the existent, are again inherent in the existent. The teleological factor is again evident.

While we have already discussed the relationship between reason, cause and action in great detail, we must apply one part of that argument to the question of explanation. The question we raise is this, is explanation itself ever causal? Only in a double sense. First, explanation has its premises for knowing in the existent. Otherwise, with what would the mind have to work as it goes about finding the explanation and working it through for the self? Secondly, explanation becomes causal in the sense that when the mind knows, it has experienced meaning; this means it has been able to explain what once was unknown to itself. Since experience experiences experience, and ideas learn from ideas, and knowledge is based on knowledge, to explain may serve as the means of bringing into being more knowledge.

There is a logical nature to cause; certainly this is true with respect to First Cause, and may be true if the human mind adheres to the intention of First Cause as it intends second cause to move on a logicality which will assure the human being the ability for experiencing meaning.

The logicality of which we speak is one which takes into consideration conditions which may change what first only appears logical. Seemingly, it is logical that I walk up the front steps, one step at a time. However, this morning a kitten was sleeping on the third step. I would say, if I am to maintain a pure logicality, I must step on the third step which would mean stepping on the kitten. A new condition now confronted me; I found it more logical, because I did not want to step on the kitten (the moral element) to jump from the second to the fourth step.

Logicality is an hypothesis which carries its own conditions; to change the nature of any one of its conditions is to change the nature of logicality. If the kitten had not been on the step, and there was no reason why I should not step on the third step, it would have been logical for me to do so.

How do we relate all this to cause?

Our hypothesis is this. If I kick one of the legs of my writing table it will move. This explains why the table moved. The fact is also present, because it has been logically determined, that because of the light weight of the table and it is not fastened to the floor, and the kick was of sufficient strength, all of which logically assures me the table will move. Now, then, would the table always move if I kicked it? Not if the conditions were changed such as, the legs being fastened to the floor. Our point is that we have a means of explaining why the table moved, the cause of which was logically determined.

If I create a motive, this will explain why I did what was done. Perhaps the crux of our problem, then, is to ask, why was the motive created, and how? What principles governed the actual creation of the motive in the first place?

An example. How must I explain this act? The act, in itself, was quite simple. As I approached my university office this morning, I unlocked the door, opened it, crossed the threshold and then pulled the door closed with such force that one of the panes of glass in the door broke. Did I have a motive for breaking the glass in the door? In other words, was the breakage intentional? Was there a drive, perhaps subconsciously motivated to break the pane? Or, was there motive at all behind the action? Would we be correct in saying that because I slammed the door with great force, it was inevitable that the glass would break. Or, was the breakage inevitable because the glass was extremely brittle; if the glass had been of a different strength, perhaps it would not have broken.

Regardless of the explanations to this point, we can say: (1) the glass was broken because the door was slammed; and (2) I was the one who slammed the door, and therefore must have had a reason for the action; (3) there may have been a number of reasons for the glass to be broken, but the reasons (whatever they may have been) were not the motive for the action.

We make a distinction then, between reasons and the motive.

The reason I slammed the door and, as a result, broke the glass, was because of anger. The reason for the anger was because during my walk to the university this morning it started to rain. Having brought neither a rain coat nor an umbrella, my suit was drenched, and I did not have time to return home to change clothes before my lecture.

Wherein lies the motive? For what? To slam the door or break the glass? To slam the door yes, but not to break the glass. Because of anger. We pause here for a moment. Did I slam the door because I was angry? Yes. But, was it (the anger) the real reason, or was there a reason behind the reason? Yes. Why was I angry? Because my clothes were drenched in a rain shower which made me angry which made me slam the door, and because of the action of the door, the glass broke. We now ask what created the motive which resulted in the reasons for the breakage? The rain? The drenched clothing? Or, the inability, at that moment, of the mind to control its response and permit itself to become angry, thereby bringing into being the results of reason?

There is no question here; the mind-action is clear. There was movement because of a value-laden assumption. Ths assumption is this. I do not appreciate lecturing for an hour in dripping clothing. Moreover, there is the possibility of becoming chilled. Because I did not have time to change, I recognized the implications involved in continuing to wear the wet clothing. Now we come to another value-laden assumption, namely, the importance of delivering the lecture in spite of the condition of my clothing. It is at this point that motive begins to be seen more clearly. Actually, my motive was to continue on schedule and complete my task, because of its importance to me; the side effect, however, was anger, which resulted in an unfortunate incident. We might say that the anger was expressing itself in my relation to the door, and the need was to get rid of the anger by taking it out on the door. All this may be true, but it does not speak to our prime concern, namely, the creation of the concept of motive. The mind did not receive the reasons for the actions; from the motive evolved the reasons which activated themselves in different forms. It is the motive which serves as the source of explanation for the action and not the reasons.

A motive then, is the cause inherent in source explaining action. Motive and its creation is a conscious activity, moving from an epistemological basis. In other words, I was fully conscious of the importance of that lecture, which caused me to decide to lecture in wet clothing; the source of that stance evolved from a time consideration, need of the data by certain of my students, etc. While my mind was fully conscious of these factors, and I willed my prime action, at the same time the mind got out of hand and permitted other action outside the pale of control.

We wish to emphasize one more point in this connection. In the foregoing paragraph, it was stated. "I willed my prime action." In this case, regardless of consequences, I intended to lecture, and I did. I had a motive for what I did. This has been explained.

May we say that wherever intention exists, there is motive? Yes. I am sitting at my writing desk. I decide to get up and walk around the room. For a particular purpose? No. This is quite secondary. The motive was not to walk around the room, even though I may do so, but rather to get up from my chair. The cause for this intention is weariness, my action is deliberate, the source explaining that act is the uncomfortable chair, the long period of time spent in the chair, etc. Because of existing conditions, my mind created the motive to get up from the chair.

Because my mind was free to choose, the motive underlying my action was actualized. In the absence of restraints, either physical or psychological in nature, the intention of the motive was realized.

While we have discussed, in part, one problem, it has raised a host of others, such as, does not all of this simply point out that what we are dealing with here is an ethical determinism? The answer is yes. We shall look at its implications.

While we have made an approach to the problem of the apparent good, another, just as significant, appears on our epistemological horizon. It is a question already suggested and answered only in part. We repeat our question in the same way Aristotle confronted his teacher Plato.

If I decide to ride in an automobile with a driver who is not a responsible driver, because I know that he is not responsible, the logic in my power to reason is being ignored and, quite literally, I am moving contrary to what I have cognized as good. If I ride with him, I know that what I am doing is not according to reason. But, I also suggested there may be a higher degree of reason such as the good to be derived from reaching a destination on time. There is not only a higher degree of reason, but new knowledge to be considered.

Still, we have not spoken to the real problem in this theory. We now come one step closer to its solution. I have decided to slide down a hill on a sled. The hill is steep and there are many trees in the path. To pursue the plan is knowing that it is virtually impossible to slide down the hill without an accident. All the logic in my power to reason tells me not to do it. But I do it, nevertheless. Why? While the logic of reason tells me one thing, I do another. The point is, that even though I move contrary to this reason, I still will for a reason such as the attached excitement, the challenge, etc., all of which may be illogical. But it is still a reason.

Perhaps our point of contention is this one, something suggested by Locke. I know the utter impossibility of reaching the bottom of the hill unharmed, but I am determined to slide in spite of reason. The only conclusion we can draw at this point is this: to determine the meaning and significance of what we determine ethically, knowledge is not a sufficient base from which to operate.

Are we not confronted with the problem of the question of a validated morality which is the working base of the will, something which is stronger than knowledge, but which uses knowledge and is willing to heed the voice of knowledge? Moreover, it is only when the mind operates from this morality base that there is the assurance of the mind's freedom to determine the highest good.

What has been said above points out yet another problem. When we speak of the affective, cognitive and conative domains as comprising the totality of the intellective process, is there any suggestion there is something unequal in their responsibility to function as mind? In other words, are we still fighting the classical position that the cognitive domain is supreme, and the conative plays a secondary role, the affective even more subordinate? If this is what we are doing, it is simple to see the reason for many of the questions raised above. However, enough has been said to make us believe that the conative is supreme, and the cognitive plays an inferior role.

I would raise yet another problem and it is this: Is it possible to trust the affective, cognitive or conative domains, any one of which, if they stand alone and operate as an entity? Our answer is an emphatic no. Locke is correct; knowledge alone is not enough to provide an operational base for the will. What about the morality of which we have spoken? It is what comes into being when each of the three domains are weighed equally, and the communication among them is open for an internalized dialogue. We can very quickly see the weakness of William James' position when he insists on believing desire or interest to be the source when the mind decides what is good, and makes it the object of the human will. Neither desire nor interest may operate from a moral base which has been validated by a mind motivated by three equal domains, the total reason of which has decided upon the highest and greatest good. Without this validated action, good is relegated to what seems good and apparency is but a questionable object.

There is a reason for this needed morality. Morality is nothing more than a self-corrective measure, a guarantee that sense experience alone, or knowledge alone, will not epistemologically force the will to act against reason inherent in cause. Only in this sense, when there is complete freedom gained by means of the self-correctice dialog, can one say that the will is ethically determined in order to function as an ethical determiner.

In essence, ethical determinism is a logically based determinism.

What is logical determinism? Before we answer this question, we find it necessary to answer first, what it is not. Logical determinism is not fatalistic in nature, scope, and purpose. However, there is a long and quixotic history in Western philosophy which has within its intent, the propagation of this theory. If we believe that "logic alone suggests that men's wills are fettered, that nothing is really in their power to alter," then, "in the clearest sense it is idle to speak of his having a free will." "The stoics thought that the most elementary con deration of logic shows this to be true."

But, is it? Here is fatalism, pure and simple. While we have no intention of discussing this argument in detail, since it is outside our purpose, it is, however, necessary to correct the thinking of such thinkers as the stoics in order to prepare the ground for our own position. The stoics spoke of logical determinism and fatalism in the same breath. What they were saying is that man's destiny is not up to him, and whatever he does, is something impossible to avoid. Here is a pre-determinism, the something which controls every thought and action of the human being.

The Scholastics raised the question about the logicality of this position, but in doing so strayed somewhat from the real issue. What they did do, however, was to give birth to new thinking about new relationships, namely, the relationship between pre-determinism and ethical determinism. As would be expected, their concern was with the knowing process instead of from the determinism angle. Also, it would be expected that they would affirm the freedom of the will. To do so, they could not follow the pathway of the stoics so they shifted epistemological gears and preferred the proposition that man is not predetermined in what he does but, it is known by the absolute what he will do. There is no place in this position for force on the part of the unmoved Mover? The logicality in this statement rests in the shift of responsibility; man is not determined (unless he wills it) but is the determiner. Even if he determines to be determined, this does not alter the fact of his responsibility. The scholastic designation God, as First Cause and Absolute, knows what each man will do before he does it. The premise here is that God is omniscient. Knowledge of what a man will do does not carry with it deterministic implications.

Here again, we are faced with a problem. How would the scholastics deal with this proposition?

1. Something has happened.

This morning, on the way to the library, my foot slipped off the lower step leading to the entrance. Because it was dark, I had been unable to see the ice which had formed on the edge of the step.

2. It was going to happen.

In other words, because of the conditions existing, such as the ice, darkness, failure to be on the alert for such possibilities, as well as the failure on my part to step further in on the step, the accident was inevitable.

We pause to react at this point. It is only logical to assume that because I placed my foot where I did, and the ice and other conditions were existent, the result was determined. Were they pre-determined? Only in the sense that the conditions for an accident were present and if I put my foot at a certain place. No accident would have taken place if the shoe had been placed two inches more on the step. The Scholastics are saying: "and God knew it would happen." Well and good. But this does not address itself to our problem.

3. It was going to happen before it did happen.

Now we come to the sticky place in our argument. We have two reactions. If we say the fates were against me this morning, and they felt it was time to shake me up a bit, so they pre-destined me to fall, the argument is a questionable one. Because, I could have controlled the situation, so no fall would have taken place. The conditions could have alerted me to danger.

The darkness, general weather conditions, always the possibility of ice on the edge of a step at this time of the year, etc. Such an alert would have cautioned me, and very deliberately, I would have placed each foot where I had reasonable assurance that no slippage would take place.

The second reaction is this. As a determiner, I allowed conditions to determine my movements. I was not thinking and, as a result, was careless in the face of possible danger. I did not use the powers of the intellective process, and what I did was not logical; if it had been, what I did would have been logically determined, by myself, as the determinant acting responsibly.

4. Nothing is even possible except what actually happens.

We have spoken to this proposition when we said: But it was possible for something else to have taken place; in other words, no accident. We hurry to add, however, that the mind in a passive and irresponsible state, brings to pass (allows) impersonal conditions to have their way and act as determinants.

In addition, we make a shift in interpretation. To say that nothing is ever possible except what actively happens, is a statement fettered by question. It is possible for me to cross the street, enter the medical building, and visit a colleague but, it is not going to happen. Even though it doesn't actually happen, it was and is possible to do so.

5. It is never within any man's power to do anything except what he actually does.

Again, this argument has been answered.

The reader acquainted with the writings of some of our major philosophers will have recognized that the five propositions studied above, outline for us the position of Diodorus Cronus with respect to logical determinism.

His arguments are weak and inconsistent. Nevertheless, we refer to his position because of the opportunities it presents to consider one significant point. But, in making his point, he destroys the logic of his own argument. It is quite evident that his position must be labeled as Fatalism, in spite of the slight aside in his theory when emphasis is placed upon a negativism which says that it is not within the power of man to do anything except what he actually does. It would be a rewarding experience to pursue an exegetical study of this thought. We may find that we have been wrong in the placement of the fatalism label on his philosophy. But, that suggestion we would question, for the following reasons. It will aid us to follow his reasoning if we structure the argument.

1. My automobile is stuck in a snowdrift. We now call on Diodorus to explain our predicament. He tells me that I am going to get the car out of the snowdrift or, I am not going to extricate the car. (Up to this point he is quite safe in his assumptions and statement). He continues, but with a breakdown in logic. If I am able to move the car from the drift, he says, I will

do so if I call the tow-truck or not. Therefore, what is the reason for calling a tow-truck? In either case, the "outcome is already inevitable."

2. What Diodorus fails to consider, and therefore his logic is anything but logical, is that there are dependency needs in the relationship among concepts. The breakdown in his logic rests upon the idea that the car will be extricated whether or not a tow-truck is called. The dependency need is that the car cannot be pulled from the drift without the aid of the truck; this is true even if some other means are chosen, such as, twenty men pushing the car from its position in the snow. Now, we must also add that, even if the truck is called, it may not be able to pull the car from its lodging. Now, some other means must be chosen; but, this would be nothing more than playing a game of semantics.

The logic of logical determinism? Diodorus teases us with some interesting points. Another of his epistemological implications is the suggestion that every statement is either true or false. This problem is discussed in a number of places elsewhere in the book, and does not merit consideration here. While we may by-pass, for the moment, this problem, it would not do for us to ignore what was referred to above as a significant point; that is, is it possible to read Diodorus without being aware of the need to consider the factor of prediction in the logical determinism argument?

While we have addressed ourselves to the implications of prediction in its relationship to determinism on many of the preceding pages, at no point have we moved beyond some of the classical arguments of Ryle and Popper. While it is not our intention to discuss these positions at this place, there is, however, the need to consider other dimensions of the same problem. For instance, we can predict, based on specific empirical data, that it will snow within twenty-four hours. To make such a prediction, many factors are taken into consideration, all of which pertain to regulatory components of natural law. This does not say, however, that factors unknown to us at the moment, cannot change the basis for the prediction. If we wish, it is possible to label these as impersonal forces. Our concern here is with personal forces which pertain to human actions and reactions. To what degree is it possible to predict what a man will do under certain and very specific circumstances? We now have the human mind to contend with; moreover, a mind not determined by impersonal forces but, which will react in such a way to indicate that it is a self-determiner.

Perhaps we should allow Aristotle to confront us with his thinking. We ask of him, Is it possible to predict the future voluntary action of a man? Aristotle answers by saying: Yes, but the prediction will always be false in the sense that since he is free, the actions themselves might or might not be performed. Our response to this might be: Doesn't the concept of prediction take what is and what might be into consideration? Why is it necessary to suggest a falseness just because an alternative exists? There will always be a rigidness for each alternative; if he chooses one alternative, the prediction pertaining to that choice will be correct, unless, of course, there is a change in the prediction. The same is true if the other alternative is chosen. For Ryle to beg the problem by substituting the words correct and incorrect does not change, in the least, our working hypothesis. Moreover, there is no reason why a prediction cannot be called true if this is the way it turns out. The prediction loses its structure when it is actualized, for the future is meaningless as a concept until it becomes the present.

Here again we must not confuse our thought processes by injecting the idea of pre-destination or pre-determinism, or the part of an absolute being, simply because He knows what is going to happen in the future. This is merely fore-knowledge, and does not suggest that the Absolute becomes the cause of something happening, serving in the capacity of a determiner, against which the human mind has no means of recourse.

Prediction does concern itself with what we might suggest as possible existence. It is possible that I may decide to visit Oxford tomorrow. In one sense, all is in order. Passport, funds, plane schedule, freedom of lecture schedule, etc. However, if I predict whether or not I shall go, it is very questionable, for a number of reasons, all of which, however, could be overcome. In each instance, the predictive statement pertaining to the possible is true. In every prediction there are alternatives; what actually occurs is what determines if the prediction pertaining to a specific alternative is true or false, correct or incorrect, if we are charitable.

What I am saying is that predictions remain as potentialities (actualities, of course) but, as an existent realized, the status is changed.

How simple it is to predict, that because of certain road conditions, and the close proximity of two cars, an accident would occur. But, it didn't because of a very small dry spot on the road which permitted the wheels to stop, and the immediate reaction of the driver to this variable. The alternative was always present, and it is not to be thought of as something of an existent past which changed matter or, of a future that was not meant to be.

Now, then, is it possible to predict what the human mind will or will not do? Here is the pivot of our problem. To speak of what the human mind will do, addresses itself, in part, to the question of human knowledge. Upon what does this depend? Our power of reasoning? Upon moral judgments? Is it possible to answer these questions without first asking, What is the relationship between determinism and moral responsibility?

Determinism and moral responsibility? Bed partners? Many epistemologists would say how strange!

It has not been our intention to speak of determinism in general terms. Here is a concept which must be defined with a great deal of specificity. For example, determinism is a term which can be applied to what happens when natural law acts. It can reveal itself in pure chance. Or, it can be the action of and by a free mind in process of determining itself. Regardless of the connotation, it is a concept very much a part of human thought and life. It is one of the main characteristics of the human thought pattern.

While the subject of moral responsibility has been discussed in detail, it is our one purpose here to posit an assumption. Since some type of determinism is an inevitable characteristic of the human thought pattern, it is our contention, in the first place, that determinism (in whatever form it takes) is compatible with moral responsibility. This presupposition, in turn, is based on the premise that the human mind is responsible for its actions regardless of the type of confrontation addressed to the mind by means of the what of determinism, even if the mind is determined by pure chance, but allows for alternatives and choice. As evidenced in our discussion on moral responsibility, only the free mind can be held responsible for its actions. One point to be made on behalf of this argument is that while something may happen, by pure chance, to the mind, the happening itself is not the action we are considering, because it is beyond the control of the mind but, rather, every action possesses implications for the mind; it is the way in which the mind reacts to these implications which does concern us and forces to the surface the need to study, very carefully, the relationship between determinism and moral responsibility.

1. All choices imply an inherent freedom of mind to select, from alternatives, what the intellective process recommends for the epistemological benefit of the total being of mind;

2. The above assumption implies that in every confrontation, (object to subject) there are implications resident in the possibilities for growth and development;

3. These possibilities now become secondary causes in their own right, making it possible for the mind to freely choose, as subject, in a way in which it functions as a self-determiner, as cause itself.

In testing these assumptions, are we suggesting that we feel uneasy about saying that determinism somehow does not fit our conception of the real structure and responsibility of the mind? On the contrary. Kant's causality of freedom is a volitile concept, only, however, when we say that determinism must be applied to the human thought pattern. And because it is very real the mind must, in its processes, be always ready to handle its moral obligation.

CHAPTER SIX

DECISIONS

The point of much of our discussion has centered on the question of the voluntary action. To answer the question we have taken a look at its counterpart, the involuntary action. All of this has forced us to define the concept of deliberateness. And now we must posit the next logical question, namely, what is the relationship between decision, action, and deliberation?

This is an important step toward completing our epistemological mosaic. For now we are confronted with the need to ask about the importance of making a decision and the necessity of knowing the ingredients of the process which brings the decision into being. This means, we are asking, what happens when a decision is being made, as the mind functions to bring about this action?

I have decided to return a book to one of my colleagues whose office is at the far end of the campus. The decision has been made. I am voluntarily making the trip to return the book; he has told me, on many occasions, he is not in need of its return. My action is deliberate; I feel now is the most opportune time for the action.

Before we proceed with the discussion, we call attention to two words, deliberate, deliberation. My action is deliberate, because I fully intend, within moments, to make the journey across campus. But, have I deliberated upon the action? It is true that when I arrived in my office this morning, the thought had not occurred to me to perform such an action. But, when I saw the book on my desk, the thought did come, Perhaps this is the best time to make the return. Because I used the word best, within a moment I had drawn a number of comparisons, fully indicating deliberation.

Now let us ask, supposing the decision was made on the spur of the moment so to speak, are we then to suggest there was no deliberation in this case? Or, we may ask the same question, Is there a type of decision for which the mind does not prepare itself in one way or another? You respond by saying, The involuntary action. Perhaps, but we may be forced to question even that statement. The important point here is to determine whether there is action by the agent, or something which happens to him. If there is action by the agent, even though it may be reflexive in nature, the mind in this instance is still operational and has its say as the total organism reacts. Is there not a process of mind deliberation whenever the total organism has been affected and the mind is operational? Is it possible to perform or act, the total organism using itself, without directives emanating from the mind? To suggest otherwise is to deny the integral and intra-dependent relationship between mind and body. Is it possible to isolate the mind totally from the ways it functionally expresses itself in sense experience? While it is true the mind uses itself to analyze itself and its functions, is the body able to perform the same feat without the use of brain and mind? Is it possible to make a decision unless the brain has taped and placed in the storage of the unconscious a factor relevant and applicable to the decision itself?

Herein lies a deliberateness based on a deliberation already made ready for withdrawal, perhaps resident in the unconscious for a long period of time. There is no difference between this and if I should have asked myself: Isn't this is a logical time, this morning, to return the book? And so, I begin to dialogue with the self and posit arguments for and against the action.

It must be remembered that when the book was first loaned to me, the decision was made first, to return the book and, secondly, to do so as soon as I had completed the reading of it. You ask, have I ever considered alternatives to this action? My answer is, No. Of course, this has affected my decision. All variables do. In a sense, then, every decision made is based on a number of other decisions, already made. Here are examples of what we mean by deliberateness and deliberation.

We have suggested the place of intention and its relationship to decision. The same has been true about the nature of conditions and how decision is affected by its intentions. Thus, we are brought to the place of asking, Do decisions have a cause?

There is a questionable logic in the position of Hampshire and Hart when they say:

> "He has not yet decided what he will do" entails "He does not yet know what he will do.". . . . If a man does claim to be able to predict with certainty his own future actions, basing his prediction on induction, then he is implying that the actions in question will be in some sense, or to some degree, involuntary . . . If it is up to him to decide what he is going to do, then he must still be uncertain what he will do until he has made a decision or until his intentions are formal . . . The certainty comes at the moment of decision, and indeed constitutes the decision, when the certainty is arrived at in this way, as a result of considering reasons, and not as a result of considering evidence.

Their stance is clear insofar as the problem of uncertainty is concerned. If it is up to the agent to decide what he is going to do, then, he must still be uncertain what he will do until he has made a decision or until his intentions are formed. The certainty (of action) comes at the moment of decision, and indeed constitutes the decision. Now the argument becomes ragged when they continue the sentence by saying: . . . when the certainty is arrived at in this way, as a result of considering reasons, and not as a result of considering evidence.

Here is another good epistemological trick if it can be done. I am interested in finding out how reasons can be considered, known or even studied apart from their characteristics as evidence.

What is being asked here is this. Is it possible to make a decision without considering reasons or, at least being aware of reasons? Do not reasons constitute evidence? Is it not logical then, to insist that all decisions have a cause? The cause now becomes the consideration or awareness of the evidence (reasons) for performing an action as well as the movement of the will which is, essentially, the actual doing of the act. Nothing is ever done until it is willed by the intellective process. The key concept here is cause. Inherent in any cause is a relationship which constitutes the totality of antecedents, namely, what went into the formation of the consideration and awareness as mental acts constituting the step-by-step, logical progression of the intellective process in its determination of the validity of the reasons being looked at as evidence? This is what we mean by the causal relationship and its responsibility for a decision.

But, of course, we may be confronted by many kinds of problems here. Earlier I spoke of knowing reasons. I appended to this the idea of the agent knowing reasons as evidence, before making a decision. It is Hume who forces us to look at a conceivable problem.

This morning, at the completion of a tutorial, I made a reading assignment, and asked the student to complete the reading of a particular book before our next session. Now he is a capable and conscientious student, a hard worker and, in my two years of tutorials with him, there has not been a single occasion when he has come unprepared. There are time factors here which carry an importance of their own. First, I had given him an assignment, a part of a contract, a part of the meaning for our relationship, which he readily accepted. Second, I know him as a responsible person who, unless there are conditions which will not permit him to complete the reading (such as extreme illness) I have every reason to believe the assignment will be completed.

All of this is evidence that it is logical that he will read the book. This is something I know. In this sense I know what his decision is before he makes it. It is reasonable to assume then, that he will complete the assignment.

But, only under the above conditions do I know what his decision will be. Only if those conditions are not changed can I maintain a degree of certainty pertaining to his actions. The causal relationship has been held constant if the conditions have not been changed.

However, my knowledge is never certain in this instance. Even though he is the most reliable of students, conditions may change such as the desire to attend a series of musical concerts, something towards which he has been looking, with anticipation, for months. And, because of the press of other work, and the decision to attend the musicals, the assignment is not completed.

There is cause, and the causal relationships are evident. Another decision now superceded the decision to do the assigned reading, one which held even greater value for him. The book could be read tomorrow, the concert will not be repeated.

Any decision which is reached always implies that if different conditions were to exist another decision may have been made. My deduction of what I might expect from him was based on a knowledgeable generalization, but also knowing that many things may happen which may cause him to break the line of logic which characterizes him without the presence of variable conditions. It must also be remembered that for the agent to know what he will do, is to control the conditions of the causal relationship. Decision is caused when conditions are finalized and considered in terms of their implications. This implies that this agent is knowledgeable about these implications.

Is certainty in decision a certainty when the agent knows what he will do because the conditions of the causal relationship are controlled?

Jacques Maritain has alerted us to the implications of what he calls the degrees of knowledge. The problem of certainty in relation to decision making requires an insight into the epistemological premises of both the degrees of knowledge and certainty in knowledge. For we must ask the question, At what point is there certainty with respect to a decision? When the mind acts upon its decision? Only then? Or, would we be willing to concede the possibility that because there are degrees of knowledge and degrees of certainty, so there are degrees of decision? Or, does this really beg the question? Doesn't the epistemological stance of the word connote a decision already reached? If I am certain that I shall return a book to a colleague today, it implies that I have made up my mind to do so; if I don't return it, there is some reason why I don't do it, such as becoming ill and forced to return home. But, all this does not affect the certainty of the decision at the time it was made. This picture can be changed almost completely if I say: I am almost certain that I shall return the book but, because of an extremely busy schedule today, I may not find the time to do so. We are now confronted by a recognized uncertainty, one which, at this point in time, takes into consideration the possibility that I may not be enabled to fulfill my plans.

Recognized uncertainty makes it its business to be aware of possible roadblocks, of all kinds, which may stand in the way of completing a legitimate intention.

Again, we ask the question, this time with different emphasis, Are there degrees of certainty? If there are, there is nothing certain about certainty. Rather, are there not degrees of uncertainty pertaining to a decision? Rather than degrees of decision? Here is an epistemological folly of which we must be aware. Moreover, such questions place directly before us the need to ask about intentions. Recently the question was asked of me, Would I accept the chairmanship of a particular policy making committee? I replied with a tentative yes. There is a degree of uncertainty about my decision because of a conflict in time with another commitment. The uncertainty rests on a recognized factor, a time conflict. If the conflict can be resolved, I intend to accept the post. My intention prepares my way for making a decision. My decision will be reached after the intention has been actualized by resolving the problems which gave meaning to it in the first place. When the offer was first made, and if there were no problems affecting my decision, there is no question but I would have accepted the appointment. But, because I recognized a problem, which would have to be resolved, and because I sought to resolve it indicates that I intend to accept if the roadblocks are removed. Intention is a significant factor here in our discussion.

To speak of certainty (without the degrees of uncertainty) and decision (without the degrees of decision) is to speak of a finality which is equivalent to an act. Doesn't all of this imply that decision and its certainty must at a point in time, be considered separately from the act which, in a sense, actualizes the decision?

Perhaps it is being suggested that to raise this question is to toy with words. If I am undecided about accepting the post of chairman, I am certainly uncertain, all of which implies an indecision on my part.

But, isn't there a certainty within the idea of indecision which erases the uncertainty factor? My indecision rests upon a conflict in time: I fully intend (I have made up my mind to do so, if . . .) to accept the appointment. Here is a certainty couched within conditions which alone create the uncertainty. The uncertainty arises because I do not know if the conflict can be resolved.

Uncertainty takes on a different connotation when it is related to a lack of knowledge of specific conditions rather than to intention. In this case there is no uncertainty about intention; now it moves from shall I accept it or shall I not? to I shall accept it, if . . .

We move to another premise. What if I say: I don't know if I will accept it or not? There is no intention here. There is indecision in a broad as well as in a strict sense. There is uncertainty. The uncertainty in this case may be due to a simple refusal on my part to even consider the question at this time. And nothing more. Nevertheless, it is a decision not to make a decision. The uncertainty rests entirely upon the factors present when the consideration does take place. The methodology used by the mind, in this instance, remains the same.

If I say: I don't know if I will accept it or not, is to imply an unwillingness on my part to make a prediction.

There are two senses in which this can be considered; in the first place, in recognized uncertainty I may hesitate to predict my decision and action. Since it is a time problem, and there are a number of conflicts for that time space, I may have to decline the offer, unless . . . the meeting time of the committee is changed to give me more flexibility. The issues to be resolved are complicated, with many side issues beginning to surface. I know that I cannot accept the chairmanship unless they are resolved. Moreover, I am aware of the nature of the major problems involved in the decision. Always moving from an empirical base, I could, if I so desire, predict, from what I know of the membership of the committee, that if I cannot resolve the time problem from the standpoint of my personal schedule, they will make a change in meeting time. These are reasons which my mind is able to validate and suggest that it is going to become possible for me to accept the appointment.

In the second place, if my reaction to the invitation is not one which is willing to consider implications, my attitude may be superficial, and I do not take seriously the need to make either a prediction or the actual decision, perhaps wanting for a more opportune time and circumstance.

Are we saying then, that the source of the morality of a decision lies in whether or not we are willing to predict what a decision might be, because it indicates whether or not we are: (1) willing to consider the implication of both prediction and decision, and (2) willing to consider all hard core facts which pertain to the decision itself and will affect, in one way or another, the intention? The answer is yes.

Intention, recognized uncertainties, implications all have an important part to play in the how and why of making a decision. In this sense there is the moral element which is an important ingredient in decision making.

The committee has honored me by offering the appointment. It is evident they have their reasons for making the offer. I, too, must make use of reason as I respond; my response is to be a careful reasoning of all evidence which will assist me in making the final decision. My interest in the work of the committee, what it is I can bring to the work of the committee must be a part of the consideration. These are factors which I have considered in reaching the decision with respect to the intention. To reason out the conflicts in time remains. If this can be done, I will actualize the intent and accept the offer.

If there is the moral element resident in the decision, it is an indication that the critical eye of the mind has been permitted to function, and this means that what is being done, as it is being done, is, at the same time, being validated. It is only in this way the mind shows its sense of responsibility by its willingness to answer for its own decisions.

BIBLIOGRAPHY

Adler, A.,	*Understanding Human Nature.*	Greenberg.
Alexander, S.,	*Space, Time and Deity., 2 Vol.*	Dover.
Ardrey, R.	*The Territorial Imperative.*	Atheneum.
Aristotle,	*Complete Works of Aristotle.*	Oxford.
Arieti, S.,	*The Will To Be Human.*	Delta.
Assagioli, R.,	*The Act of Will.*	Penguin.
Augustine, St.,	*City of God.*	Penguin.
	Confessions.	Dutton.
Austin, J. L.,	*Philosophical Papers.*	Oxford.
Ayer, A. J.,	*Language, Truth and Logic.*	Dover.
	The Problem of Knowledge.	Macmillan.
	Logical Positivism.	Allen and Unwin.
	Philosophical Essays.	St. Martin's Press.
	The Foundation of Empirical Knowledge.	St. Martin's Press.
	Russell.	Fontana.
	Russell and Moore.	Harvard University Press.
	Metaphysics and Common Sense	Macmillan.
Ayers, M. R.,	*The Refutation of Determinism.*	Methuen.
Barron, F.,	*Creativity and Personal Freedom.*	Van Nostrand.
Barth, Karl,	*The Epistle To The Romans.*	Oxford.
Bartlett, F. C.,	*Thinking.*	Allen and Unwin.
Berdyaev, N.,	*The Destiny of Man.*	Harper & Row.
	The Meaning of the Creative Act.	Collier.
	Space and Reality.	Bles.
Bergson, H.,	*Time and Free Will.*	Allen and Unwin.
	Creative Evolution.	Macmillan.
	The Two Sources of Morality and Religion.	Macmillan.
Berkeley, G.,	*The Principles of Human Knowledge*	Macmillan.
	Philosophical Writings.	Nelson.
Berlin, I.,	*Four Essays on Liberty.*	Oxford.
Berofsky, B.,	*Determinism.*	Princeton University Press.
	Freewill and Determinism.	Harper and Row.
Block, M.,	*The Importance of Language.*	Prentice-Hall.

Bolton, N.,	*The Psychology of Thinking.*	Methuen.
Boole, G.,	*An Investigation of the Laws of Thought.*	Macmillan.
Bourke, V. J.,	*Will in Western Thought.*	Sheed and Ward.
Bradley, F. H.,	*Appearance and Reality.*	Oxford.
	Collected Essays.	Oxford.
	Essays on Truth and Reality.	Oxford.
	Ethical Studies.	Oxford.
Buber, M.,	*Between Mind and Man.*	Macmillan.
	I and Thou.	Clark.
Cassirer, E.,	*An Essay on Man.*	Yale.
	The Problem of Knowledge.	Yale.
Chiari, J.,	*The Necessity of Being.*	Paul Elek.
Church, R. W.,	*A study in the Philosophy of Malebranche.*	Kennikat.
Collingwood, R. G.,	*The Idea of History.*	Oxford.
	Essays on Metaphysics.	Oxford.
Copleston, F. C.,	*Aquinas.*	Penguin.
	A History of Philosophy.	Doubleday.
Craik, K. J. W.,	*The Nature of Explanation.*	Cambridge University Press.
Croce, B.,	*Aesthetics.*	Peter Owen.
Davidson, M.,	*The Free Will Controversy.*	Watts.
Descartes, R.,	*The Philosophical Works., 2 Vol.*	Cambridge University Press.
Dewey, J.,	*How We Think.*	Heath.
	Resconstruction in Philosophy.	University of London Press.
	The Quest For Certainty.,	Allen and Unwin.
	Logic.	Holt.
Dufrenne, M.,	*The Notion of the A Priori.*	Northwestern University Press.
Enteman, W. F., (ed).,	*The Problem of Free Will.*	Scribner.
Evans, C. O.,	*The Subject of Consciousness.*	Allen and Unwin.
Farber, L.,	*The Ways of the Will.*	Basic Books.
Farrer, A.,	*Freedom of the Will.*	Humanities Press.

Frankl, V. E.,	*Man's Search for Meaning.*	Beacon.
Franklin, R. L.	*Freedom and Determinism.*	Humanities Press.
Freud, S.,	*The Future of an Illusion.*	Doubleday.
	Introductory Lectures on Psycho-analysis.	Allen and Unwin.
	Psychopathology of Everyday Life.	Penguin.
Fromm, Erich,	*The Art of Loving.*	Barnes and Noble.
	May Man Prevail.	Doubleday.
	Man's Concept of Man.	Ungar.
Gardner, P.,	*The Nature of Historical Explanation.*	Oxford.
Hampshire, S.,	*Thought and Action.*	Viking.
	Freedom and the Individual.	Harper and Row.
	Freedom of Mind.	Princeton University Press.
Hare, R. M.,	*Freedom and Reason.*	Oxford.
Hegel, G. F.,	*Phenomenology of the Mind.*	Macmillan.
	The Philosophy of History.	Oxford.
Heidegger, Martin,	*Being and Time.*	Harper and Row.
	Existence and Being.	Regnery.
	The Question of Being.	Twayne.
Hume, D.,	*A Treatise of Human Nature*	Oxford.
	An Enquiry Concerning Human Understanding.	Oxford.
Husserl, E.,	*Ideas.*	Macmillan.
James, W.,	*Principles of Psychology. 2 Vol.*	Macmillan.
	The Will to Believe.	Dover.
Jaspers, Karl.	*Man in the Modern Age.*	Doubleday.
	Three Essays.	Harcourt-Brace.
	General Psychopathology.	Manchester University Press.
	Reason and Existenz.	Noonday.
Johnson, E. E.,	*Logic. 3 Vol.*	Dover.
Jung, Carl.	*Psychology and Religion.*	Yale.
	The Undiscovered Self.	Routledge and Kegan Paul.
Kant, Immanuel,	*Prolegomena.*	Barnes and Noble.

	Critique of Pure Reason.	St. Martin's Press.
	Critique of Practical Reason.	Bobbs-Merrill.
Kenny, A.,	*The Anatomy of the Soul.*	Blackwell.
Kierkegaard, S.,	*The Journals.*	Oxford.
	The Concept of Dread.	Oxford.
	The Concept of Irony.	Collins.
	Either/or.	Princeton.
	Fear and Trembling.	Oxford.
	The Sickness Unto Death.	Doubleday.
	Concluding Unscientific Postscript.	Oxford.
	Purity of Heart.	Harper.
Köhler, W.,	*Gestalt Psychology.*	Bell and Sons.
Lange, J.,	*Cognitivity Paradox.*	Princeton University Press.
Lehrer, Keith (ed),	*Freedom and Determiniam.*	Random House.
Leibniz, G. W., von,	*Philosophical Writings.*	Dutton.
Levi-Straus, C.,	*The Savage Mind.*	University of Chicago Press.
Locke, John,	An Essay Concerning Human Human Understanding.	Macmillan.
Lonergan, B. J. F.,	*Insight.*	Philosophy Library.
Lorenz, K.,	*On Aggression.*	Harcourt, Brace and World.
Lucas, J. R.,	*The Freedom of the Will.*	Oxford.
Luther, Martin.	*The Bondage of the Will.*	Eerdman's.
Mabbott, J. D.,	*An Introduction to Ethics.*	Hutchinson.
Marcel, Gabriel,	*The Mystery of Being. 2 Vol.*	Regnery.
	Being and Having.	Harper and Row.
	The Philosophy of Existence.	Harvill.
	Homo Viator.	Harper and Row.
Maritain, J.,	*The Range of Reason.*	Scribner.
	Creative Intuition.	Princeton.
	An Introduction To Philosophy.	Sheed and Ward.
Marcuse, H.,	*Studies on Critical Philosophy.*	Beacon.
	One Dimensional Man.	Beacon.

Maslow, A. H.,	*Motivation and Personality.*	Harper and Row.
May, R.,	*Love and Will.*	Norton.
Mead, G. H.,	*Mind, Self, and Society.*	University of Chicago Press.
Meldon, A. I.,	*Free Action.*	Routledge and Kegan Paul.
Merleau-Ponty, M.,	*The Phenomenology of Perception.*	Routledge and Kegan Paul.
Mill, J. S.,	*A System of Logic.*	Longmans.
Monod, J.,	*Chance and Necessity.*	Collins.
Moore, G. E.,	*Principia Ethica.*	Cambridge University Press.
Morgenbesser, S. and Walsh, J. (ed),	*Free Will.*	Prentice-Hall. Kegan Paul.
Mortimore G., (ed).,	*Weakness of Will.*	St. Martin's Press.
Nietzsche, F.,	*Beyond Good and Evil.*	Random House.
	The Birth of Tragedy.	Doubleday.
	Thus Spake Zarathustra	Allen and Unwin.
	The Will To Power.	Random House.
O'Connor, D. J.,	*Free Will.*	Doubleday.
Pascal, B.,	*Pensées.*	Hachette.
Pears, D.,	*Wittgenstein.*	Fontana.
Pfänder, A.,	*Freedom of the Will.*	Macmillan.
	Phenomenology of Willing and Motivation.	Northwestern University Press.
Piaget, J.,	*Genetic Epistemology.*	Columbia University Press.
Plato.	*The Dialogues, 2 Vol.*	Random House.
Polanyi, M.,	*Personal Knowledge.*	Routledge and Kegan Paul.
	The Study of Man.	Routledge and Kegan Paul.
	The Tacit Dimension.	Routledge and Kegan Paul.
Popper, K.,	*The Logic of Scientific Discovery.*	Basic Books.
	The Poverty of Historicism.	Harper & Row.

	Conjectures and Refutations.	Basic Books.
	The Open Society and Its Enemies.	Princeton University Press.
Price, H. H.,	*Thinking and Experience.*	Hutchinson.
Ribot, Th.,	*The Diseases of the Will.*	Open Court.
Ricoeur, Paul.	*The Symbolism of Evil.*	Beacon.
	Freedom and Nature.	Northwestern University Press.
Royce, J.,	*The World and the Individual. 2 Vol.*	Dover.
Russell, B.,	*History of Western Philosophy.*	Simon and Shuster.
	Human Knowledge.	Simon and Shuster.
	Our Knowledge of the External World.	Humanities Press.
Ryle, G.,	*The Concept of Mind.*	Hutchinson.
Sartre, J. P.,	*Situations.*	Fawcett.
	Being and Nothingness.	Philosophical Library.
Schopenhauer, A.,	*The World as Will and Idea.*	Routledge and Kegan Paul.
Skinner, B. F.	*Beyond Freedom and Dignity.*	Knopf.
Spinoza, B.,	*Works, 2 Vols.*	Dover.
Stevenson, C. L.,	*Ethics and Language.*	Yale.
Teilhard de Chardin, P.,	*The Phenomenon of Man.*	Collins.
	The Divine Milieu	Collins.
	Human Energy.	Collins.
	The Future of Man.	Collins.
	Hymn of the Universe.	Collins.
Weiss, Paul,	*Man's Freedom.*	Southern Illinois University Press.
	Modes of Being.	Southern Illinois University Press.
	Nature and Man.	Southern Illinois University Press.
Wertheimer, M.,	*Productive Thinking.*	Tavistock.
Whitehead, A. N.,	*Symbolism.*	Putnam.
	The Aim of Education.	Macmillan.

	Process and Reality.	Cambridge University Press.
	Adventures of Ideas.	Macmillan.
	Science and the Modern World.	Macmillan.
	Modes of Thought.	Macmillan.
Wittgenstein, L.,	*Tractus Logico-Philosophicus.*	Routledge and Kegan Paul.
	Philosophical Investigations.	Blackwell.
	The Blue and Brown Books.	Blackwell.
Young, J. Z.,	*An Introduction to the Study of Man.*	Oxford.